Somebody's Got My Hymnal

John Yarrington

Remember Bethany's 50th and the missing hymnal!

Happy Father's Day! 2004

Marion

Abingdon Press
Nashville

SOMEBODY'S GOT MY HYMNAL

Copyright © 2004 by Abingdon Press

This book is printed on recycled, acid-free paper.

Scripture quotations are from the New Revised Standard Version of the Bible, copyright © 1989 by the Division of Christian Education of the National Council of the Churches of Christ in the USA. Used by permission.

ISBN 0-687-08097-5

04 05 06 07 08 09 10 11 12 13 — 10 9 8 7 6 5 4 3 2 1

MANUFACTURED IN THE UNITED STATES OF AMERICA

Contents

Introduction

So many of you loved *Somebody's Got My Robe* because the title alone immediately resonated with you. I guess this book is the equivalent of "Robe II" because I still have some things to say to you. I've added a few choir types, for example.

The Wanderer

This actually happened at First Presbyterian Church. An alto, processing into a divided choir loft, turned right (not left) and followed her husband, and all the rest of the men into the pulpit side of the choir loft. Problem? She was the *only* woman there. She looked puzzled, then simply made a gallant march across the chancel to her rightful place.

The Gallactically Stupid

There, there, be calm. In the movie *A Few Good Men,* one of Tom Cruise's great lines to his associate, who has blown it and who is now offering advice, was "Thanks for your comments from the gallactically stupid." I experienced this phenomenon at a recent Christmas concert involving two adult choirs, one children's choir, and a forty-piece orchestra, all of which rehearsed in the sanctuary on Saturday morning before the service Sunday evening. Upon entering the rehearsal room Sunday evening, the first question was "Do we sit like we sat yesterday at the rehearsal?" Several responses raced through my brain, but fortunately I simply said "Yes."

Here are some possible answers (the ones that raced through my brain):

- "Please sit with someone you really like. Oh no, don't worry about the vocal part."
- "It really doesn't matter because we are going to run

down all of the aisles and simply swarm into our places."

- "The orchestra will be in the way—ask them, please, to move."

The Dis-rober

"May we take off our clothes when we wear our robes? It is SO hot up there in the choir loft."

Possible answers:

- "Does this require music?"
- "What if someone yells 'fire!'? "

So, gentle reader, the saga continues. We love these folks who come to people our rehearsal rooms and our choir lofts, don't we? Where would we be without them? Even after all these years, I still find great joy in working with volunteer singers. They come in many different sizes and shapes and many are "wonderfully different."

My scene is a bit different these days. I direct the choral activities at Houston Baptist University, where I audition singers and rehearse more than once a week. Imagine! Then, on Thursday, I take myself down to the First Presbyterian Church, where I have the privilege of directing the best church choir I have ever had. I go to no meetings. I set no goals. I never "retreat" with the staff. If I so much as see a piece of butcher paper and magic markers, I run from the room! But, gentle reader, I *have* done all of the above for many, many years, and in all that time I believe in this calling of "church musician." I love my work at Houston Baptist University and I am blessed to have a wonderful choir bunch downtown to make my life complete.

CHAPTER ONE

"I've Got the Blue Jeans Blues"

"Music is well said to be the speech of angels."
— *Thomas Carlyle*

"There are more bad musicians than there is bad music."
— *Isaac Stern*

"There is no doubt that the first requirement for a composer
is to be dead."
— *Arthur Honegger*

The title of this chapter has to do with, of course, the proliferation of services to reach the unchurched and the demands placed on what music is to be played and sung. In his book, *Beyond the Worship Wars,* Tom Long states: "Music is the nuclear reactor of congregational worship. It is where much of the radioactive material is stored, where a good bit of the energy is generated, and, alas, where congregational meltdown is most likely to occur.[1]

This is a hard time for musicians in the service of the church. With Elijah, we might sing, "It Is Enough," or perhaps join in with the words of that famous Bach cantata, "Ich habe Genug," for which the Yarrington translation is, "I've had it!" We who are classically trained are being asked to take leadership of bands, screens, praise songs, scripture songs, and the like. What we value in music, liturgy, and hymnody, we are told, does not reach the unchurched. Away, then with the hymnal! Away with the organ and the robed choir! It's blue jeans and lightly disguised Broadway show tunes that draw people to our sanctuaries. Forget seasons, color, and symbols! These are unfamiliar to those in the newer generations. God forbid that someone should instruct these "faithful" in the articles of the faith.

Is this an overstatement? Hardly! In a later chapter, "four-letter" words are discussed. There is certainly one four-letter word that applies to this discussion and that is the word *fear*.

- The pastor fears being left behind in the church growth movement.
- Older parishioners see what they value and with which they feel comfortable thrown out the window. They feel invaded and fearful.
- Younger worshipers want something more culturally attuned to them in music, liturgy, and dress. Leaders fear that "they" won't come unless we court them in these ways.
- A classically trained music minister cannot, in all cases, adapt to these new influences and is fearful for his or her job.
- Parents want their kids "churched" and taken care of, even "fixed" in some cases. They live in fear of drugs, pregnancy, and ruined lives.

I am continually distressed when I hear the voice of dear friends who are experiencing all the pressures inherent in this discussion and who are, for the most part, the kind of "servant-musicians" of whom Dr. Harold Best speaks in his book, *Music Through the Eyes of Faith*. They feel called to ministry and most are willing to adapt and bend, but often they are called to break. What they hold dear (sacred) in music, hymnody, and liturgy is called into question. Their training is called into question. They feel like dinosaurs walking on a strange and hostile planet.

Here's the news! YOU ARE NOT ALONE!

Voices from Baylor

At Baylor University this past spring a church music workshop was held, underwritten by Billy Ray Hearn, a Baylor alumnus, noted musician, producer, and promoter. Hearn is chair of EMI Christian Music Group and the founder of Sparrow Records. How wonderful it is that he took the initiative to make the event happen. He also understands the current scene. "What's happened is, the ministers of music or the worship leaders have not been trained to do what they are being asked to do now. . . . The job schizophrenia music ministers increasingly experience comes from unrealistic expectations and pressures." [2]

Dr. William V. May, dean of the Baylor School of Music, agrees with Hearn and is most sympathetic.

They've [church musicians] found themselves embroiled in the church wars. Churches have divided over these issues. In those places where it has become genuine conflict, where congregations have literally divided, then it's even more tragic. The whole issue of worship style has overshadowed the real mission of the church to the degree that people succumb to human frailty, put the worship of God out of the picture and put all of their own personal prejudices in place. [3]

Dr. Donald Balmos, another Baylor alumnus and music minister at Seventh & James Baptist Church, adjacent to the Baylor campus, has an even blunter assessment of the current state of affairs.

Ministers of music, as they are currently trained, may become a prehistoric animal. They will need to become not just choral musicians, but musicians who understand jazz/pop elements as they apply to church music, musicians who understand instrumental music as well as they understand vocal music.[4]

Baylor Magazine, from which this material is excerpted, states that recent surveys confirm these observations. *Christianity Today* magazine commissioned a survey that revealed a significant trend in church worship styles. In 1992, "traditional" was the dominant form of music in more than 50 percent of all U.S. churches. By September 2001, that number was down to 24 percent. Another 22 percent of the churches characterized their music as "contemporary." The biggest gain, 43 percent, was found in the category called "blended," describing services that incorporate both traditional and contemporary music styles.

Finally, Dr. Terry York, author of America's *Worship Wars*, says that the source of the conflict is part of a "shift from modernity to postmodernity as it funnels into and is played out in the sanctuary. The short answer is that what we're experiencing in worship and all the different styles of worship is warfare. What worship and warfare have in common is they are both the ultimate in human expression." [5]

A Fantasy Panel

I love those newspaper articles in which one gets to suggest a guest list for dinner. I thought that might work in this chapter as we ponder where we are in church music and where we might be going. So I've asked the following to be on my fantasy panel.

> **Dr. Thomas Troeger, author of** *Trouble at the Table*
> **Marva Dawn, author of** *Reaching Out Without Dumbing Down*
> **Harold Best, author of** *Music Through the Eyes of Faith*

Dr. Y: Dr. Troeger, you tell a most interesting story about going to a park to relax one afternoon and seeing in succession: a young couple with guitars, singing folk music; a fine arts group with a large boom box playing classical music; college students throwing a Frisbee to country-western music; and a van marked "Hard Rocker." Your comments were revealing.

TT: "Bird song, splashing water, and the wind in the trees were lost to colliding rhythms and a general cacophonous rumble. I felt surrounded by alien tribes: the folk tribe, the classical tribe, the country western tribe, and the hard rock tribe. Each group turned up its volume as the others arrived so that staying near the source of their sound, they did not have to listen to the competition. So I got up and walked away, but as the great cacophony of musical tribes faced in the distance, there arose in my mind the memory of all the different kinds of music that members of congregations want sung in church."

Dr. Y: How would you define "tribe"?

TT: "A tribe is a primary kinship unit drawn together by common interests, values, and goals. We feel most comfortable when we are with our own tribe. We know its customs, its peculiar character and allegiances, its beliefs and rituals, its symbols and code words, its particular ways of celebrating and being together." [6]

Dr. Y: I know I speak for many when I thank you, Marva Dawn, for your writing about the current scene. Certainly, everyone has read *Reaching Out Without Dumbing Down*, but I found some help for this discussion in your book *To Walk and Not Faint: A Month of Meditations on Isaiah 40*. You used Isaiah 40:9 as a basis for the chapter:

> Get you up to a high mountain,
>   O Zion, herald of good tidings;
> lift up your voice with strength,
>   O Jerusalem, herald of good tidings;
>   lift it up, do not fear;
> say to the cities of Judah,
>   "Here is your God!"

You contemporized the text as, "Broadcast it from the mountaintops, you people of God, couriers of the good news. Proclaim it in every way, you saints who are messengers of this good news. Shout still more, don't be afraid. Say to each and every one who dwells in your land, 'Look! Your God is here!' "[7]

You continued to speak in this chapter about how information is disseminated. You made the bold statement that "faithful evangelism cannot be programmed." What does that mean?

MD: "Churches try so frantically to institute evangelism programs or evangelistic worship services (which is a confusion of adoring God and speaking to the neighbor, to the detriment of both) and forget that our witness takes place within our daily lives, in ordinary interactions and loving relationships. The Greek text of the Great Commission literally says, 'While going, be making disciples of all nations' " (Matt. 28:19). [8]

Dr. Y: In a later chapter of this same book, you speak about the advancements in media technology. Could you speak to this?

MD.: "I grieve for young people in their twenties and thirties—and even more for the elementary students my husband teaches—who have had have no family interaction, no relational activities in their homes, because everyone is too busy watching television or playing with the computer. The statistics on time for family intimacy are appalling, with spouses spending less than five minutes per day with each other and less than half a minute with their children in conversation. Such behavior, common in U.S. culture, leaves huge holes of yearning in people's lives. And how will the church fill those gaps with the love of God and the love of the Christian community?

"I sometimes feel immobilized because churches seem to be failing so badly to offer the Truth of God that our culture so desperately needs. Instead I see clergy grasping for gimmicks to attract the world, studying marketing techniques to make their congregations appealing, reducing worship to entertainment instead of genuine praise of God and formation of the character of believers and the community." [9]

Dr. Y: Dr. Best, your book *Music Through the Eyes of Faith* is, for me, a clear statement of what church music could be. You speak of the "quality of crafting," in an early chapter, could you elaborate?

Dr. B: "The quality of the crafting (of the music) will be determined by the degree of technique and skill the maker possesses. Technique and skill are closely connected: technique is the facilitator and skill is the degree and refinement of the facility. Yet creativity, technique, and skill often get mixed up with each other in the musical world. The making of music does not always signal the presence of creativity. If I am creative, I imagine a different way of music making than someone else would. I must then possess the skill to execute the difference. If I can only duplicate someone else's music making, I am not creative but merely skillful. If my imitation of someone else is third-rate, then neither skill nor creativity is apparent." [10]

Dr. Y: You also speak of authentication relative to creativity and music making.

Dr. B: "We should not make music in order to prove that we are or to authenticate ourselves. God created in us the capability for understanding that we are authenticated in him, not in what we do. In the final analysis, music making is neither a means nor an end but an offering. Therefore an act of worship. All music makers everywhere must understand this and proceed accordingly. Nothing but harm lies ahead if we try to authenticate ourselves with our musical works or become so attached to them—addicted might be a better word—that we have no sense of worth or being without this 'proof' of our existence."

Dr. Y: I believe this quote from your book is the most profound statement regarding this whole discussion:

Each musician must come to experience the dignity, rightness, and eventual joy of putting things aside, of emptying oneself and taking the form of a servant. Such musicians must be able to move back and forth, gracefully, servingly, and willingly, from the symphony to the folk tune; back and forth without complaint, compromise or snobbery, without the conceit that doing an oratorio is somehow more worthy or more deserving than doing a hymn tune. All servant musicians must be able to be in creative transit, serving this community and challenging that one, all the while showing grace, power, elegance and imagination.[11]

A Hospitable Community

In my book, *Somebody's Got My Robe*, I discussed the idea that having an attitude of hospitality is critical to music ministry. Here are some suggestions that will help your music ministry serve as a hospitable community within the worshiping congregation.

1. Avoid using words like "good" and "bad." These words come with a lot of "freight." Try "appropriate." When we use the "G" or the "B" word, we set ourselves up as the arbiter of taste. As we attempt to raise standards, we find ourselves raising hackles instead. If we function as "servant-musicians," we can let the needs of the entire congregation guide our choices.

2. Know your hymnal. Often pastors echo the famous statement by Victor Borge: "I know two tunes, one is 'Clair de Lune,' the other isn't." If you really know your hymnal you can make suggestions in a supporting way. Once a pastor sees that you are willing to bend a bit, you might even be able to do one of those "new" songs occasionally. The appropriate question is: Who are the hymns for? Certainly not for the organist (who has an endless supply of wind or electricity), nor for the music director or, for that matter, the pastor. The hymns are for the congregation and our job is to see that they get a wholesome diet. In this regard, constantly search the new supplements and sources for texts and tunes that might work for a particular emphasis or occasion.

3. Define your role in the music ministry. Envision your role as the church's song leader. In this leadership role, be willing to make yourself available to serve the church in various ways, such as:

- Lead singing for Sunday school classes, board meetings, and so on. This seems so simple, but often we musicians are viewed as unwilling to do this type of duty.
- Church dinners, board/leadership meetings, and staff meetings are great places to lead. Use fun songs. Get people clapping, tapping, and clanging their forks against their glasses.
- Vacation Bible school is an excellent opportunity to serve through music. Being available to Sunday school teachers to help them with the music part of the curriculum is a great idea.

4. Personalize your ministry. Make it a priority to know congregational members not in the music program. I always found that taking part in the hospital rotation was more a blessing to me than a ministry to those in the hospital. For those in the music program, send notes out with all of those reminders. Birthdays, anniversaries, sports events, plays at school, and so forth, all are important moments to personalize your ministry. I guess this goes without saying, but if we really are in ministry then we want to be involved with all of our people.

5. Know the seasons of the Christian year. In addition, know something about the mores and practices of your particular denominational tribe. Look for ways to use music with the congregation as the seasons progress, not in a "teachy" manner, but to help them experience the color, flavor, and meaning of the seasons. Consider these:

- Congregational sung refrains for Advent, Christmas, Epiphany and other seasons of the Christian year
- Baptismal sung responses, communion responses
- Sung prayer responses, thanksgiving responses
- Hymn anthems
- Hymn of the month

Begin with the Music

I think it is important when approaching the congregation to begin with the music. Your voice is your strongest ally. Sing to "them" in an inviting manner and encourage them to join you. Don't talk. For goodness sake, don't tell them anything about Ralph Vaughan Williams, or any other information you deem important. Choose wisely, then expect and encourage them to join in.

Read the church growth literature so you won't be behind. Learn from this and approach these ideas with a critical eye. No one is asking us to take the growth movement as it is presented, but we should be wise about what is being written and said.

However, in all of this, you are not called to be a doormat. What do you do when you receive under your door, a bulletin from a neighbor church, with the hymns circled and the note, "We should sing some of these." Signed, "Your Members." There is something about an anonymous note that sets the blood boiling. You are not going to satisfy everybody. "Why don't we sing the hymns we know?" may be answered with, "What hymns do you know?" Keep an accurate list of those chosen so you know you are attempting to satisfy many needs, not just your own. Then, when someone says to you, "I hate it during Advent when you sing those dreary hymns like 'O Come, O Come, Emmanuel,'" you can sometimes just smile and go on. It is the price of peace.

Know yourself. *The Musician's Soul* by James Jordan has

much good in it. It has been a lifesaver for me. Remember, fear is at the heart of much of our problems. Here is the list again (feel free to add more "fears" that may apply to your setting):

- The pastor fears being left behind in the church growth controversy.
- Older parishioners see what they value thrown out the window and feel invaded.
- Younger worshipers want something more culturally attuned to them in music, liturgy, and dress. Robes and organs, to them, seem old-fashioned.
- A classically trained music director cannot, in all cases adapt to the new influences and often is literally cast out of a job.
- Parents want their kids churched, taken care of, "fixed" in some cases.

As I quote from those who have had profound influence on me, I am always afraid that I will not quote them sufficiently to do justice to what they say. I am one who underlines and highlights and writes marginal comments. In any author quoted I hope you will read the entire book. A part of any journey is to welcome fellow travelers. In James Jordan, I have found such a welcome friend for my journey. Here are some thoughts from *The Musician's Soul*.

The journey of this book is about one idea: you must trust, believe, and love yourself. Music making is constructed of correct notes, correct rhythms, dynamics and articulation. But the mortar of music is human trust (of self and others), belief in self and others, and love of self.

A conductor does not "conduct"; he, by the nature of his being and his spirit, causes people to sing; he evokes sounds that hopefully, are reflective of each person's individual life experiences. Granted, technique and the mechanics of conducting must be taught and respected. However, the stuff that allows for the creation of great music is rarely dealt with in the teaching of conducting. What is usually easiest learned is hardest taught. Soulfulness is a hard thing to talk about and teach.[12]

When we put all of this together, we are really speaking about opening oneself, and being vulnerable. I think this is why I so enjoyed working with children's choirs all those years in church music, because it was so possible, so easy, to be oneself and, of course, if you tried another approach, the children saw right through you. I always felt refreshed after working with them because much was new and fresh.

In a sense, many of us maintain that childlike quality of wonder, openness, and trust, sometimes to our detriment. And we are wounded and discouraged again and again because we continue to try, to invest, to love, to care. When what we value is threatened, when we are asked to function in a capacity for which we have little or no training, we are, I believe, in essence being asked to be something (somebody) we are not. The pressures are great, aren't they? And we are fearful that we won't measure up or, far greater, that we might even lose our job.

Grieving

What we have been speaking about is really a grief process. We grieve for what is lost. I encourage you to read *A Royal Waste of Time* by Marva Dawn, especially chapter 17. She pens letters to the various entities in good New Testament fashion. Here are two examples of her letters.

To Struggling Pastors

Dear Shepherd of Souls,

I know it is deathly hard for you these days to fulfill your call from God to be truly a pastor. You want what is good for the people; they want to be amused and entertained. You want to draw them away from their idolatries and they want to bring those very idolatries into the congregation's worship.

Certainly it helps us in these difficult days to keep remembering that the truth lies in the middle between two extremes. I know that you are trying to find a positive middle between these extreme poles, and I commend you for enduring the tensions.

To Wounded and Bruised Musicians

Dear Gifted Servant of Our God:

Let me thank you for your continued devotion to God's truth as you sort through new music to find the finest. Often you are being more theological than your pastor when you keep questioning some of the suggestions you are given for songs to use. What amazes me so much is that you have continued to be patient in teaching about music, even though you have been made the scapegoat for the whole congregation's failure to be outreaching.

You have heard me say this many times—the root problem of most of the churches' woes is that all of us—congregations and pastors alike—need to learn what it means to be the community that is the Church. That is why the last thing we ought to do is divide the community along the lines of worship taste. The issue is more important than that immediate problem, so all your investment of energy in trying to end the division is well worth it.[13]

Notes

1. Thomas G. Long, *Beyond the Worship Wars: Building Vital and Faithful Worship* (Bethesda: Md.: The Alban Institute, 2001), p. 53.

2. Billy Ray Hearn quoted in Robert F. Darden, "The Wars of Worship," *Baylor Magazine* (September/October 2002).

3. Ibid.

4. Ibid.

5. Terry York, *America's Worship Wars: Veterans of the Front Versus Veterans of the Fort* (Peabody, Mass.: Hendrickson Publishers, 2003).

6. Carol Doran and Thomas Troeger, *Trouble at the Table: Gathering the Tribes for Worship* (Nashville: Abingdon Press, 1992), pp. 11, 13.

7. Marva Dawn, *To Walk and Not Faint: A Month of Meditations on Isaiah 40* (Grand Rapids: William B. Eerdmans, 1997), p. 52.

8. Ibid., p. 54.

9. Ibid., p. 66.

10. Harold Best, *Music Through the Eyes of Faith* (San Francisco: Harper, 1992), pp. 12-16.

11. Ibid., p. 33.

12. James Jordan, *The Musician's Soul: A Journey Examining Spirituality for Performers, Teachers, Composers, and Music Educators* (Chicago: GIA Publications, Inc., 1999), pp. 7-9.

13. Marva Dawn, *A Royal "Waste" of Time: The Splendor of Worshiping God and Being Church for the World* (Grand Rapids: William B. Eerdmans, 1999), pp. 208-14.

CHAPTER TWO

I Come to the Garden Alone

HYMNS OF THE LUKEWARM CHURCH

1. A Comfy Mattress Is Our God

2. Joyful, Joyful, We Kinda Like Thee

3. Above Average Is Thy Faithfulness

4. My Hope Is Built on Nothing Much

5. O God, Our Enabler in Ages Past

6. Oh, How I Like Jesus

7. I Surrender Some

8. Take My Life and Let Me Be

9. When the Saints Go Sneaking In

10. Where He Leads Me, I Will Consider Following

Music is basic to the human condition. Our job, as conductors, is to help people do what comes naturally: to select, refine, and polish; to organize, enable, and encourage. We're not asking anyone to perform an unnatural act! So why do we often find ourselves in the position of taskmaster and disciplinarian, imposing our will on a reluctant ensemble or audience? Do we dominate our choirs for the sake of an artistic product, or to fortify our egos?

Joshua R. Jacobson writes, "Challenge your singers to

become more musically self-reliant; they need not abdicate all responsibility to the conductor. Demonstrate that you trust their sensitivity. Consider even allowing your large choirs to perform in concert without the constant domination of a conductor."[1]

When I needed a text for the conducting classes I teach at Houston Baptist University, after a careful search, I decided to use *Evoking Sound* by James Jordan. There were plenty of conducting treatises, most of which begin and end with pattern maps. I wanted something closer to what my teacher, Bev Henson used to teach, "Ask your choirs to do what they can do." In other words, have some faith in their ability, sensitivity, musicality, and musical intuition.

I believe I made the right choice. I discovered that Dr. Jordan's book is about how one achieves sound from a work in an evoking frame of mind. It is much of the same philosophy espoused in the previous quote. Also, I must tell you that the quotes at the beginning of each chapter, a Jordan "trademark," are worth the price of the book.

My advice to you, as you read this chapter, is to run, not walk, to purchase *Evoking Sound*. I do not exaggerate when I say that his insight, wisdom, and vulnerability—his ability to open himself up to others—has given me the freedom to be myself and to conduct my choirs with relationship in mind. I have had times when I was not at all sure that my interest in people, my passion for relationships, was really the way to achieve an artistic product. I am now convinced that, for me, it is the way to go.

The quotes I use from various authors all suffer from incompleteness and I worry that, taken out of context, they may not be as meaningful as I wish. Join me in being an underliner, highlighter, and margin writer. I come back again and again to texts that are meaningful to me and I can only hope that you will read these books in their entirety. Let the quotes in this book whet your appetite for much more!

We Do Not Come to the Garden Alone

My story is pretty simple. From age six, I played the piano seriously. My mother, going about her daily chores in the kitchen, would yell in to me, "B-flat! That's a B-flat!" or "That rhythm is not clean." Needless to say, I excelled at the piano and, more than that, I developed a lifelong love for music. Growing up, I thought that everyone listened to opera on Saturday afternoons—blasting from large speakers with your father joining in on most of the tenor arias. I thought everyone practiced a couple of hours before going to high school in the morning. I confess that I am a dud at those parties where you play games based on the popular music of your time. My "popular" music was opera, symphony, and all the piano literature I was learning. I also had a valuable and enriching musical experience through the church from children's choirs on up. I was fortunate to have a wonderful lady, Ruth Fowler, who inspired, educated, cajoled, and held up the highest standards of the choral art. I was blessed with George Smith at Will Rogers High School, whose passion for singing well is still my passion, all these years later.

After receiving a Bachelor of Music Education degree and because of the strong influence of Dr. Orcenith Smith, I went to Union Theological Seminary for two years, studying for a Masters in Sacred Music. He was also instrumental in landing me my first job at McFarlin Methodist Church in Norman, Oklahoma. It was there I studied and received an "advanced" degree, the Doctor of Musical Arts.

Why do I tell this? We all have our stories and memories of people who exerted great influence on us. We haven't done anything in our musical journey entirely by ourselves. We really don't come to the garden alone.

Balancing Ministry and Artistry

My struggle, all these years, has been between the demands of ministry—that is to say, relationships with the people who actually sing and play; and the demands of artistry—correctness, style, balance, and intonation. There has been tremendous tension in this journey for me. How about you? I believe that the demands of ministry do not have to be sacrificed on the altar of good choral "performance" and, likewise, the demands of the highest degree of the choral art can coexist with ministry. It's just that we must recognize that the tension inherent as we walk this path is enormous.

Volunteer singers in a choir, after all, are quite a wonderful breed. They volunteer to come on Wednesday or Thursday (or both) and again on Sunday. They commit to sing in worship regularly. They go on retreats, slop spaghetti for trips, and constantly give feedback—subtly and not so subtly. One of the problems is that they sometimes "volunteer" the wrong pitches or rhythms, and often "volunteer" to show up for Sunday service without attending the rehearsal *for* the Sunday service!

Let's face it, the more we ask for crisp consonants, beautiful vowel sounds, phrase shapes, color, and passion, the more some suspect that we are on an ego trip to satisfy ourselves or to demonstrate that we are truly the best. There is a confused mentality from some who are suspicious of work that delves below the surface. In this regard, we often hear the notion that "performance" is a bad word. Let me pause and bring in a dear friend, Roger Deschner, who has departed this life, but left a legacy of the kind of teaching and inspiration so valued by many of us.

An ill-thought out cliché has been on the lips of many church musicians. (And, I add, choir members.) They say our choirs do not "perform," nor do our organists, instrumentalists, and soloists. To them, performance is a bad word.

The problem is that "performance," at root, has never had that crass meaning. We need the word in talking about church music; God uses the word in making demands on our choirs. It must be salvaged. If we are talking about "selfish uses of church music," then that's what we should say, and that temptation to misuse church music must always be held to the light. But God asks us today in our choirs, as God has always asked that we give our best "performance," that which we have carefully prepared for God's use.

/Performance simply means to complete what one has set out to do, to accomplish it with the special skills that are required. Performance asks us to take the time to complete through preparations for an anthem./Performance asks us to hone our skills so that a more perfect gift can be offered to God and our neighbor. Performance demands commitment, time, work, and a willingness to use our talents. The opposite of good performance is half-done, half-learned, misunderstood, shoddy, ragtag offerings of music in worship that too often afflict us and must embarrass even a caring, forgiving God. Shoddy offerings are signs of a lack of faith and commitment. Good performance arises out of our faith and love of God.[2]

There! I feel so much better. So where does that leave us? If you have been in the service of the church's music very long, you know that the tensions can be pretty severe—especially in light of the current scene. What one word describes the nub of our discussion? It's already been mentioned in the first chapter. It's a four-letter word. It's the word *fear.*/Fear that we are not as capable as someone else. /Fear that we don't care enough./Fear that our skills and training will not be needed much longer./Fear that if we ask for more commitment and dedication our folks will not like us and will stay away. Fear that our anger over some of the stupidity afflicting the church will spew forth when we least expect it. So, what do we do?

In an excerpt from *The Musician's Soul* (remember, run, don't walk to this book) Peter J. Gomes gives the following healing word:

Fear, not sin, is the great curse. Fear that I'll be recognized for the fraud that I am—the great imposter complex. Fear that I will fail in some worthy endeavor or fear that I will succeed in some unworthy enterprise. Fear that I will not have enough time to do what I must. Fear that I will hurt or be hurt. Fear that I will not know love. Fear that my love will be painful and hurtful. Fear that the things that I most believe and trust are not so. Fear that I am untrustworthy. Everyone of us is hostage to fear. [3]

Let's face it, folks. Church is often the place where you receive the least hospitality, and the most hostility and criticism. Church is where someone wearing a hateful expression pulls you aside at the fellowship time and asks, "Can the organist play softer?" My answer is, "Yes." Let that go. You're not going to win that one! Or, you spend weeks working with that "uncertain singer" (don't you just love that term) in your children's choir, and after the children sing in a service, someone asks, "Did you know you have someone singing too low?" My response, "No, I didn't. But thanks for bringing that to my attention." My wife would tell you that that's not my real response. A religious publisher cannot print the real response! Don't you just want to scream, "I have spent hours with that kid, and sometimes he is on pitch. But he's as much a part of the choir as the best singer. All the kids know he's not on pitch yet, but they are helping in the process. He's not a 'crow' and I'm planning to have him sing *every* time the choir sings, for you see, *he is more important than the product!*"

I guess that notion really summarizes my philosophy, theology, methodology, and other "ologies." Persons are more important than the product.

Does this mean that we "allow" anything in the name of ministry? Bad vowels, sloppy consonant articulation, out-of-tune singing, and/or inattention to text sense and shape? If someone says, "I just gave my singing to Jesus," as a reason for a half-hearted, badly sung attempt, my response is, "Do you know what Jesus would say?" I believe he would say, "Take it back!" All right! Simmer down. My tongue is firmly in my cheek.

Teachers and Prophets

We are, after all, teachers and, in many cases, prophets. Yes, I said, "Prophets!" You are a prophet when you hold up for the choir their responsibility in leading the congregational hymns as their priority over and above anthems or oratorios or musicals. Imagine that concept! You are a prophet when you attempt to teach, with the choir's help, unfamiliar hymns to a congregation mostly happy with "what they know."/After all, "I know what I like" usually really means "I like what I know."

In a former church, I was intent on teaching unfamiliar hymns. My approach was friendly, hospitable, and expectantly positive. I used an offshoot of the Texas phrase, "Shoot first, and ask questions later." I found that if I approached the congregation as if offering a gift, asked them to join, gave them time to do so without instant criticism, that, for the most part, they would come along. I remember teaching "Come, Christians, Join to Sing" (SPANISH HYMN) to a United Methodist congregation. The hymn was new to the denomination's hymnal and to my congregation. Someone stopped me a few months afterward to remark, "When you teach those new hymns, I just close my book." I responded, "I noticed that you were singing, 'Come, Christians' this morning and I'm curious about that." The response? "Oh, that's one we already know!" Interesting! Because that hymn was not in the former book used by this congregant. In spite of that closed mind and book, the hymn had seeped into their repertoire.

In the book, *The Courage to Teach,* Parker J. Palmer says:

Teaching, like any truly human activity, emerges from one's inwardness, for better or worse. As I teach, I project the condition of my soul onto my students, my subject, and our way of being together. The entanglements I experience in the classroom are often no more or less than the convolutions of my inner life. Viewed from this angle, teaching holds a mirror to the soul. If I am willing to look in that mirror and not run from what I see, I have a chance to gain self-knowledge—and knowing myself is as crucial to good teaching as knowing my students and my subject. [4]

What I am going to suggest to you is really very simple but I think it is very important. Choir directors need, in a word,

FUEL! I believe that we are not alone when we take time to read the Bible and pray daily. I always have some other devotional guide as well because I need it. I pray for people by name and the list changes. I always pray for me, that I may be up to the challenge. Constant reading of books and periodicals keeps me sharp. I want to know what others think and how they solve problems. Observe other rehearsals. Attend workshops. Develop and foster relationships with individual choir members. Care about them. Know about them. Send handwritten notes.

Stick to your guns, you must know where you are taking your people. And don't be deterred by the "naysayers." They will always be with you. Some people who sing are unhappy. You care, but you cannot, in all cases, take care of that. They will know that you genuinely care and that is what is important! Don't sell "them" short. "They" will come up to you after a particularly difficult anthem or cantata and say, "I really didn't like that piece at first, but I really like it now."

That you care does not mean for one moment that you do not intend to maintain your goals and standards. You return from one of those workshops all aglow with enthusiasm and ideas, and two of your basses sit on the back row with arms folded. Their message is clear: "Don't bother us with this new stuff. We've seen this before. You will gradually wear down. If not, we will see to it ourselves." This is not mean at all, but it is reality as I have experienced it. We grow when we entertain new ideas, read new books, seek out an outstanding teacher and they grow also, even if you have to carry them bloodied and beaten toward the promised land. You can accomplish it with love and care. One-on-one-on-one you will lead them forward. It takes courage, fortitude, dedication, prayer, and the willingness to open yourself up to them. Or, to quote Parker J. Palmer again:

> Knowing my students and my subject depends heavily on self-knowledge. When I do not know myself, I cannot know who

my students are. I will see them through a glass darkly, in the shadows of my unexamined life—and when I cannot see them clearly I cannot teach them well. When I do not know myself, I cannot know my subject—not at the deepest levels of embodied, personal meaning. I will know it only abstractly, from a distance, a congeries of concepts as far removed from the world as I am from personal truth." [5]

Notes

1. Joshua R. Jacobson, the Massachusetts ACDA *Choral News*.

2. Roger Deschner, *Your Ministry of Singing in the Church* (Nashville: Discipleship Resources, 1990), pp. 13-15.

3. Peter J. Gomes quoted in James Jordan, *The Musician's Soul: A Journey Examining Spirituality for Performers, Teachers, Composers, and Music Educators* (GIA Publications, Inc., 1999), p. 29.

4. Parker J. Palmer, *The Courage to Teach: Exploring the Inner Landscape of a Teacher's Life* (San Francisco: Jossey-Bass, Inc., Publishers, 1997), p. 2.

5. Ibid.

CHAPTER THREE

Knowing the Score

A band director named Ravelli was having a lot of trouble with one drummer. He talked and talked and talked with the drummer, and performance simply didn't improve.

Finally, before the whole band, he said, "When a musician just can't handle his instrument and doesn't improve when given help, they take away the instrument, and give him two sticks, and make him a drummer."

A stage whisper was heard from the percussion section: "And if he can't handle even that, they take away one of his sticks and make him a conductor."

* *

The first graders were attending their first music lesson. The teacher was trying to begin at the beginning. She drew a musical staff on the blackboard and asked a little girl to come up and write a note on it. The little girl went to the blackboard, looked thoughtful for a minute and wrote, "Dear Aunt Emma, just a short note to tell you I'm fine."

As a beginning doctoral student, I thought I was a pretty good writer. After all, I had had many articles published in several choral magazines, and my work with the church newspaper, week after week, had obviously honed my skill. So, I turned in my first written work at the University of Oklahoma with high hopes. My paper was returned with the following in red: NOT SUITABLE FOR UNIVERSITY COMMUNICATION. I subsequently learned a very different style of writing—"suitable" for not only university communication, but also for a more professional world than that of the church newspaper. The professor in this class used a phrase I have appropriated for my own: "Writing clarifies thinking." I do not believe anyone teaches or conducts well without thorough score study. I don't know how one teaches effectively without the discipline of asking the right questions of a particular piece.

Getting to the Heart of Music Making

At Houston Baptist University I discovered that my students really didn't know how to look at a piece of music. In order to rehearse, you must know something about form, style, harmony, text, and accompaniment. You start from the big picture, the large form, and work inward. For a three-minute anthem as well as for a major work, we exercise a rigorous discipline that enlivens the teaching aspect of our work and frees us from having to look down again and again at the score. The old adage reminds us/"Have the score in your head and your head out of the score."

Since this is a choral art, beginning with the text is the basis for any analysis. I fear that, when we teach a piece of music, we often just "sing through it" with little regard for textual implications. This manner of thinking asserts: "Let's learn the notes and rhythms and let the conductor supply the interpretation."

It is a misunderstanding to see the page as a basic source of information that, if followed exactly, will yield a usable product. (Imagine a recipe, followed exactly, with no care for the freshness or flavor of the ingredients.) To "improve" the product, one can't just add a few seasonings. One has to go back to the beginning with new ingredients and a new focus: flavor *first*, not last.[1]

We place too much emphasis on the notation, which, at best, can only show us about 40 percent of the whole. This is not to advocate a "feeling level" approach (I chose this tempo, this piece, and am doing it in this way because I "feel it" this way). I insist that my students sing every line of every part of the piece they are to conduct. How can they ever possibly know what is being sung, if they, themselves, don't experience it? I insist that we focus on text, speaking it for meaning, listening to the rise and fall of syllables, and attempting to get to the musicality of the text itself, apart from any musical considerations. How else, for example, does one teach and conduct Gregorian chant? The rhythm of chant is the rhythm of the text, pure and simple. We begin a piece like Lauridsen's "O Nata Lux de Lumine"[2] by speaking the text musically, warmly, and with feeling—giving attention to the rise and fall of the words, followed by intoning or chanting the text on a unison pitch. By doing this, we immediately go to the heart of music making.

Coming to Grips with the Page

Ann Jones speaks of "coming to grips with the page." I have outlined some of her suggestions here.

1. Know what the pitches are. This process begins with playing and singing through each line, circling or checking any mistakes you make. As you do this, ask, "How does each line work? How do the lines interrelate?"

2. Know accurate rhythms. As you work through this process, vitalize the subdivision. Aim for precision.

3. Note where good intonation might be faulty. Circle awkward voice leading and intonation problem places.

4. Note the proper dynamics. Rehearse under the dynamic at times. Adjust the balance as written, and shift or add voices appropriately.

5. Note difficult diction problems. Know how to communicate correct diction to your singers.

6. Determine the appropriate style. Remember that what is on the page doesn't represent performance practice.

7. Devise an exercise to treat a particular intonation problem. Explain what you are doing, then go to that place.

8. Devise an exercise to treat a particular rhythmic problem. Again, explain what you are doing, then go to that place.

9. Remember that people learn in a variety of ways. Some learn aurally (hearing the music), and some learn visually (seeing the music).
10. Create a rehearsal plan.[3]

Dr. Jones also suggests an outline for structural analysis that includes overall form, subsections, bar groupings, scoring, key signature, time signature, score memorization, and rehearsing structurally. I have heard her say many times: "The most important decision you make is tempo." That includes acoustics, harmonic rhythm, and a speed at which the smallest details may be heard.

James Jordan echoes some of these ideas in *Evoking Sound:*

1. Hum or moan through the piece. Breathe for as many entrances as possible.

2. Play and sing all parts individually. Then, play one part and sing another until all combinations of parts have been experienced.

3. Reinforce Alexander-based alignment sensations and thoughts.

4. Mark the score. The key to score marking is to establish a consistent procedure.

5. Conduct while humming or moaning through the piece.

6. Study and experience the breath of the piece carefully. It is important to have a clear sense of where the choir will breathe within phrase structure and between phrases.

7. Conduct the piece while inhaling and exhaling constantly.

8. Breathe the color of the style and affect of the piece.

9. Study and experience the breath process that connects phrases. When teaching a piece, take special care to teach how the breath begins simultaneously with the end of the phrase.[4]

If you are saying to yourself, "this sounds like a lot of work," you are correct. Someone once asked Robert Shaw, "Mr. Shaw, how much do you score study?" His reply: "All the time." We simply cannot expect to teach well, conduct expressively, or prepare our choirs to approach a level of performance with all of the musicality inherent in their task, if we don't first study. We have no right to stand in front of "them" without this careful, studious preparation.

My own score marking is relatively simple:

/1. I look at text, circling important (Alice Parker calls them "weighted") syllables and marking breathing.

2. I look at the overall structure, marking phrasing with a solid vertical line. On first look, I like to make check marks where I think the phrasing is before committing to a solid line.

3. I study key centers and harmonic rhythm.

/4. Where change occurs is a fundamental principle. Why it occurs is equally important.

/ 5. I mark dynamics with only two colors: red for loud and blue for soft. (I told you this was simple.) *Crescendo* is marked with red, *decrescendo* with blue. I often use yellow highlighter for specific markings of tempo or color.

/ 6. If the text is in a language other than English, I write in the translation. The singers also need a written translation, side by side with the English.

7. I also like to include, in my printed copy, any pertinent information about the piece or its composer.

After this preparation, I am able to conduct either without score, or simply have the score there for reference. Remember, if I twitch, grunt, bend, sway, mouth words, move my body around, I can't hear "them." If I have to look in the score all the time, my error detection is hampered, but, more than that, I cannot evoke sound because I am too busy looking to see where I am. My tendency is to overmark, especially regarding articulation. I offer these ideas not as a system as such, but to help you see the value of careful, systematic score analysis. It will free you to make music with "them."

Notes

1. Alice Parker in *Melodious Accord 2* (June 1995).

2. Morten Lauridsen, "O nata lux de lumine," *Lux Aeterna* (New York: PeerMusic, 1997), arrangement for SAATTBB voices, *a cappella*.

3. Ann Jones, from unpublished seminar notes.

4. James Jordan, *Evoking Sound: Body Mapping Principles and Basic Conducting* (GIA Publications, Inc., 1996), pp. 165-68.

CHAPTER FOUR

"Same" Is a Four-Letter Word

TOP 10 REASONS FOR JOINING THE CHURCH CHOIR

10. You're running out of clean clothes and the robe saves on laundry.

9. The church is usually crowded and you want to make sure you always have a seat.

8. You've just been selected for jury duty and you want to get used to sitting with a large group of people.

7. The collection plate is never passed to the choir.

6. There's a clock in the back of the church and you want to know when one hour has passed.

5. You've always wanted to know who sits in the back of the church but were afraid to turn around and look.

4. You've been known to nod off during the service and don't want the minister/priest to catch you.

3. The pastor cannot look right at you during the sermon, so you never have to feel guilty.

2. The chairs for the choir are padded and are the most comfortable chairs in the church.

1. Actual singing is optional!

In conducting classes at Houston Baptist University, I often ask the question, "Why do you choose this tempo, this articulation, this dynamic—even, this piece?" In other words, "Why do you conduct *this* piece in *this* way?" The wrong answer is, "Because I *feel* it that way."

Why is that the wrong answer, one might ask? Is it wrong because it does not serve the music well? When one operates by "feel," one is conducting in "la-la land." Does this negate the power of intuition? Can one in every instance actually give exact rules for what he or she wishes to hear? Of course not. Our job, however, is to serve the music well and that can only happen by asking the right questions. So, where style is concerned, *feel* is also a four-letter word.

Too much music is made on the "feeling" level, particularly in church. Tempi become capricious. *Accelerando* and *ritardando* become a thing of the moment rather than an integral aspect of the whole. *Crescendo* and *decrescendo* are inconsistently rendered. Then, there is the matter of text. Often, we teach notes and rhythms and then add text. Result: a b-o-r-i-n-g, unmusical, "notey" outcome.

And what of phrasing and form? Do we teach our people to sing toward a destination (the end of the phrase), recover, and do it again? Often, we beat the notes into "them" and seldom plumb the musical depths. I have even heard the statement made, "I've worked on the notes and rhythms, now I'm going to put in the music." In the words of that popular song, "Too late, my brother." "Too late, my sister."

Rehearsing Is a Holistic Endeavor

I have learned that my students really don't know how to look at a piece of music to see what makes it tick. They fail to apply what they are learning in theory, history, literature, private voice, and ensemble. Rehearsing, for me, is a holistic endeavor in which all of the elements of the piece are in play. One does not get "correct" notes and rhythms and then put the music in. From the beginning, one encourages the spirit as well as the mechanics of the piece. So much music I hear is "correct" and extremely dull (another four-letter word). It needn't be this way.

Is it dangerous to listen to recordings? I don't think so. What is dangerous is to imitate someone else. Study first, away from the piano or recording, read something about performance practice, then go to more than one recording for inspiration.

The same piece of music sounds completely different when different musicians bring their knowledge and experience to its consummation and recording. The choices regarding performing forces, tempo, articulation, style, and use of language result in different "interpretations" of the same work. That is, I believe, where we church musicians should be.

This does not mean that we perform a "masterwork" every Sunday. Robert Wetzler published a collection called *Blizzard Anthems* for those times we all experience when the weather is actually fine, but the performing "forces" are few in number. It does mean, however, that we are on better ground if our choice of literature and our method of teaching and performing have come about because of our study and questioning. One brings the same serious score study to those easier, more serviceable anthems as to the bigger pieces. One develops a way of looking at any piece to make the teaching more interesting and the singing more musical. We should always ask: "What kind of piece is this?" In the family of musical style, does it belong to: chant, psalter, chorale, folk, romantic, contemporary, or pop/rock?

Was this text chosen because: (1) It is meaty, profound and deep; (2) It represents the theology of your church; (3) It is appropriate for a specific time in the liturgical church year; (4) It serves the function of a "special" day or event; or (5) It amplifies the theme of the service, the scripture for the sermon or underlines the mood (or all three)?

Even if you have chosen a "feeling" type of anthem that serves the above criteria and that, if the truth be told, is neither meaty textually nor bold musically, one still needs the following elements to be in place: (1) good tone; (2) well-formed vowel sounds; (3) consonants that give flesh to text understanding; (4) tuned chords; (5) care with dynamics; (6) phrasing and destination places; and (7) high points.

And always, dear reader, when speaking of our choices of anthem, solo or hymn/"appropriate" is such a much better word than "good" or "bad." It is less pejorative and judgmental and puts you in position to present a balanced program of music that serves, comforts, satisfies, instructs, and challenges (imagine!) the tastes and needs of your wide-ranging congregation.

The notion that we "offer" only that which is immediately accepted negates any chance we have to be prophetic in our music making or sermon giving. "I know what I like," usually means, "I like what I know." According to Marva Dawn, we can indeed reach out without dumbing down. Many churches are offering multiple worship experiences most successfully. But to suggest, as many have, that traditional anthems and hymns have no place is to take a stance that dismisses the fathers and mother of our faith in past years and forces everyone to like one type of song. Is this easy? No! Is it worth it? Yes!

Music Making in Mezzo-land

So, we come to that four-letter word—*same*. That is, same tone, same dynamic, text (all words weighted equally), same *legato* singing without lift or articulation. One writer says we dwell mostly in "mezzo-land." I believe this relates not only to dynamics, but also to all of the various qualities going into music making. Possible reasons we "perform" with a *same*-ness include:

1. We are not really sure about the differences in families of style.

2. We are afraid to take chances because a colleague (or in the competition arena, a judge) might take exception.

3. Perhaps we are actually secure in performance practice matters, but woefully inadequate in knowledge of vocal or choral growth and health.

4. We "program" for our colleagues.
5. We are slaves to the page.

Well, gentle reader, you see where this is going. We are not sure about differences in style practice because we have not taken time to read, listen, and question. We like to be *safe* (another four-letter word) and thus, we are satisfied if we get most of the notes and words right. Often we don't know enough about the voice and how it operates and so we simply yell at our choirs: BLEND! BLEND! BLEND! PHRASE AND SUPPORT! SOPRANOS—YOU'RE FLAT!

The beginning concept of a piece means that I must find a way to interest "them" and inspire "them" to take a leap of faith with me in learning a "new" anthem. Every aspect of that initial introduction concerns itself with color, nuance, shape, sound, phrasing, articulation, textual meaning, and emphasis. How does this happen?

The Notion of Sight Reading

Sight reading or sight singing is a learned, skill level endeavor that involves pitch and interval recognition, rhythm, and text. To ask a volunteer choir to "read through" a new piece often accomplishes the following:

1. The few who are at all capable of reading at sight are challenged and excited.

2. Meanwhile, on the back row, Elmer the bass is lost—completely, totally lost. Verna, in the soprano section, is singing loudly with tonal and rhythmic indifference. Susie (the questioner) already has her hand up before you have gone two measures and the organist has turned not one, but two pages. Many are "volunteering" to stay too long, to start late, to take valiant but totally inaccurate leaps at melody and/or interval and you, O mighty director, are in front, surveying the fray. Text comprehension? Phrasing? Word shapes? Forget it!

Does your choir like this new piece after first reading?

Probably not. You have two choices: (1) Choose easy music based on a well-known hymn, with little attention to how it sounds—dwelling, not in Beulah Land, but in mezzo-land; or (2) Lead them in a specific process to enable them to find the music in the anthem.

- Ask "them" to speak the text, not in the rhythm of the music, but in the rhythm and idea of the poetry. If the text appears on a facing page, so much the better.
- Encourage them to speak in a midvoice range and remind them that this is not a punishment for past sins (though they be as scarlet).
- Stay longer on important words or syllables and do not allow unimportant words, such as *the, two, of, and, or* to achieve prominence. In other words, begin with text. If you have chosen well, this will be attractive and will pay dividends.
- Get them to listen. Ask one section to speak a part of the text and everyone else listen. Reverse the procedure. This difference approach will seem very slow to some. What is actually happening, of course, is that we are dealing with one aspect of the music at a time. In this case, text.
- Think of as many ways to vary this routine and resist the temptation to put yourself into the interpretation. Let them find their way a bit. Encourage them to take responsibility for their part of this.

Learning the Music

1. Sing the music. Start with the melodies of the piece, everyone singing on a neutral syllable. Make learning the music a game or competition. For instance, you can throw the melody back and forth (antiphonally) around the room. Use your own voice as a model inflecting what you sing with all the color, sound, and nuance you can muster. LISTEN TO THEM. Did they come close to what you modeled? Go back and try again—always encouraging them, never scolding. Exaggeration is a good tool. Singing "before" (bad) and "after" (good) is also fun. Keep the process moving and let the accompanist help—*lightly*.

2. Mark the music. Take the pledge: PENCILS ARE A SIGN OF INTELLIGENCE. Mark breathing. Mark unaccented syllables with a dot or in parentheses. Show destination of phrase with a downward arrow over the important word or syllable or underline it.

3. Put it all together. Now, try a run-through. Encourage them to keep going. Don't allow them to sing unmusically, even if they miss a few notes. Use rehearsal time to work out problem spots and solve problems.

CHAPTER FIVE

"I Dance . . . They Play"

Hymn Quotes from Kids

1. God bless America! Through the night with a light from a bulb!

2. Give us this day our deli bread!

3. Glory be to the Father, and to the Son, and to the Whole East Coast!

4. We shall come to Joyce's, bringing in the cheese!

5. Gladly, the consecrated, cross-eyed bear.

6. Bringing in the Sheets

7. Dust Around the Throne

8. Praise God from whom all blessings flow, praise him all creatures, HERE WE GO!

9. While shepherds washed their socks by night.

10. He socked me and boxed me with his redeeming glove.

A famous orchestra conductor was asked about conducting, and he is supposed to have replied, "I dance . . . they play." I have two strong reactions to that statement. (Imagine?) First, the idea that "they" play is substantial. When we get over our "maestro-mentality" and our need to control what goes on musically; when we trust our singers and players and give over to them some of the responsibility of the music making; when we trust *their* musical "inner voices" as well as our own—then, we enable, evoke, and allow music to be made at the highest level.

Robert Shaw once remarked in a rehearsal, "Some things are just too wonderful to conduct." Did he mean that he let his singers and instrumentalists vote on tempo, style, color, or dynamics? Of course not! This is something conductors can never do. What we can do is to be so well-prepared, so in tune with the score, and so comfortable in our own skin, that we can afford to be vulnerable in the face of great music.

I can state today that the artistic results of my work with singers, choirs and orchestras in the opera house and on the concert platform must be ascribed . . . to educational endeavors. I think my musicians and singers will acknowledge that, far from being put under any pressure or compulsion, they were encouraged to obey their own inner urge in their playing and singing, and that my constant inspiriting served to stimulate them to give of their best in the common effort, and to participate in my intentions.[1]

Now, the second observation: if we "dance" on the podium, that is, if we move about, sway, grunt, bend our knees, clap, tap, stamp, cluck, sing along or mouth along—if, in other words, our physicality gets in the way of the music making of others, then we do a disservice to the music. Moreover, when we move excessively we can't really hear what is going on. I think the two hardest dictums for my conducting students are: (1) Stand still; and (2) Don't talk—show.

The choral conductor deals with people who are the instruments. As singers grow under the care of the dedicated and competent conductor, they develop as total physical and musical personalities. A true commitment to the music itself is thus impossible and inseparable from a commitment to the singers, to their growth both individually and corporately. Without a strong commitment to the worth and potential of the singers under his/her leadership, the love, patience and faith that are so necessary in dealing with amateur choral singers are missing in the choral conductor, to the detriment of both the singer and the music itself.[2]

The Grammar of Conducting

I am passionate about clean, clear, effective conducting. Conducting is a "skill-level" endeavor, and demands the same type of effort and technique required of anyone who masters a skill, musical or otherwise. Where did we get the idea that we simply wave around, emote, shout, cheer-lead, and our groups will respond with beautiful singing. What we should be about is the *grammar* of conducting. We have two hands. We should learn their effective use in gesture. We can learn patterns and most books are full of those diagrams but I say unto you: patterns will not save you unless "correct" is your goal. A pattern without sound is like a day without sunshine in the choral world. Does that mean it's all right to hum, sing, or grunt along with your group? No, it does not! It means that in your practice you never make a gesture without sound. You are connected to the sound. You feel it. It is palpable. It can be molded.

Conducting technique is important. This book does not attempt to rewrite what has already been said about conducting technique. This book does attempt to provide valuable insights for both novice and experienced conductors concerning the relationship between choral sound and physical gesture. This book will ask you to examine issues about yourself. It will ask you to understand movement. It will ask you to learn about your own body. It will try to shed some light on the miraculous gift of hearing music. But most of all, I hope that this text will take a step toward you trusting your innermost musical instincts, your musical "inner voice." Until you listen to yourself and to your own gifts, you will find the art of conducting will reduce itself to artless physical mime.[3]

One can save valuable rehearsal time when singers are trained to respond to clear, effective, noneffortful gesture. That conductor A may get a wonderful product by much rehearsal, exceptional musical gifts while he/she sways/grunts and sweats, does not mean that is our model to follow. If there is truly a *grammar* of conducting, then waving, swaying, mouthing, bending the knees, moving the posterior, and jumping up and down is equivalent to saying to the group, "We ain't gonna do it that-a-way." We would be laughed off the podium for that sentence and we get the same treatment for our off-the-wall, over-the-top gestures.

At Union Seminary all of us had field work jobs. I had a small Presbyterian church choir, a pneumatic organ and a pneumatic organist. I had one bass who could only sing when the bass of the organ part played what he sang. I'm not kidding! Often there was no tenor. So, I found myself directing and also singing tenor. What a concept! We assembled weekly to share our experiences. Asked if we sang with our groups, there were various answers:

- "I sing with my group because there is no tenor." (My answer)
- "I sing with my group to give them confidence."
- "I sing because I'm trying to influence the organist, not the choir, to be more musical."
- "I sing with my choir because when I sing with them—I CAN'T HEAR THEM!"

We've all been there, haven't we? In our heart of hearts, at rehearsal, we know that all of our singing, clapping, tapping, or running up and down singing *their* parts really doesn't accomplish what we hope. If we can't teach *them* to sing the anthem on Thursday, how can we hope that they will be able to do it on Sunday? Sunday, for the volunteer choir, is always a day of reckoning similar to a kamikaze mission. You've been rehearsing the same anthem for weeks. However, several were out for the rehearsal, including your two best tenors and the one bass who doesn't peal out over the rest. At the warm-up, held not in the choir room, because a Sunday school class is in that room, but in a hallway closet, several are late, two can't find their music, and one laments: "Somebody's got my hymnal!" Is it any wonder that our faith, hope, and especially charity are tested?

I used to think that I could simply pull my people through with sheer determination, grit, and sweat—especially sweat. I have learned that this standard *grammar* of conducting really works and musical results are directly proportional to beauty of gesture, precision of gesture, and the all-important breath preparation.

I am convinced that the average church choir member can actually learn to respond to your clear, concise physical direction, sans circling around, both hands flailing in the air, singing for them, clapping, tapping, and the like. Our problem is that many have not been trained to respond to these signals. As one sweet lady said to me, after I had shown how I planned to conduct a certain place in the anthem, "Honey, don't worry! We aren't looking at you anyway."

Dictum One: Stand Still

Think of your body as the backdrop to your conducting. Standing "still" does not mean stiff or unmusical. It has to do with poise, assurance, and a settling effect that enables you to hear what is really going on. We conductors would be the first to criticize a singer who moved around a lot, breathed with a high chest, and bobbed his/her head or knees because we could see that "effort did not equal good performance." The obvious reference is to our conducting. Here are my suggestions: (1) read *Evoking Sound* and get the accompanying videos; and (2) videotape some of your rehearsals. You will be amazed at how much effort you expend.

The breathing process is clearly described by James Jordan:

> Breath is the *core* of all conducting gesture, all music making. The most important element to facilitate the breathing process is to have the

body open to receive air before the breath is taken, or initiated. If you analyze any of the activities of life for which we take air into our bodies you will notice that just prior to the point at which air falls into our body, a relaxation, or opening of the entire breathing tract takes place so that the airways are open in order for the air to seemingly "drop in" to our body.

Think of releasing all the muscles surrounding your torso in order to allow breathing. Think of allowing air to flow into and out of your lungs, rather than pulling it in or pushing it out.[4]

One of the difficulties for a conductor is that we don't always have an ensemble to conduct. Your church choir can function as that for you without their ever knowing it. Practice on them. You will get better and they will get better. Keep the following practice principles in mind:

1. Always practice conducting from the same body alignment position that you will be using when you conduct.

2. Make certain that you breathe as if you were conducting, inhale for the 'preparation' to start the piece and exhale (release your breath into the sound) while you are conducting.

3. Never practice conducting gesture that is not intimately connected to sound.

4. At the very least, practice conducting with a partner to experience the music-making with another person.

5. When you conduct other persons, let the sound be your teacher.

6. Listen to the breath of those you conduct.

7. Sing and conduct when preparing musical materials for conducting.[5]

Dictum Two: Don't Talk—Show

Often, when working on an anthem, we say something like the following, "Now on page 3, sopranos remember that the B-flat needs to be higher. Basses, bottom of page 4, crisp consonants, remember to put the "t" on the third beat. Tenors, look up at the top of page 5." Sound familiar? This has the same effectiveness as announcements in church, which is to say, not much. Here are some steps that work for me.

1. Establish the "want-to" in the group. Nothing is as crucial as the initial introduction to something new. Play all the way through it or use a recording so that people get an over-all impression.

2. Begin with one element: the text *or* the tune. Speaking of text, in a musical manner, midvoice is a wonderful way to work for proper emphasis and phrasing. Destination is a crucial music-making word. How can we get there if we don't know where we are headed. Singing the tune on a neutral syllable allows focus on that aspect of the piece.

Seldom do I just "read through" an anthem. I want them to like what I have selected. I feel personally involved. We can accomplish much more by isolating elements and then beginning to put the whole thing together. Your voice is still your best teacher. Sing to them what you want. Listen to see if they gave it back to you. Sing again. Ask them to reproduce the same color, nuance, shape, they heard. Make a game of it. Most choirs like to demonstrate how badly something might sound. Encourage this. It's the before and after theory.

Ann Jones says, "engage the music maker." Play to the highest common denominator. Don't be discouraged that the naysayers, the negative, the critical weigh in. They will weigh in, but they don't have to carry the day. They are actually pretty fearful because they have limited skill and you are asking them to sing better, hold their music up, cut off together, sing in tune with tall vowels—imagine!

Meeting Mr. "Ictus"

An "ictus" is simply what happens when the downward motion of our gesture (the downbeat) changes to a reactive upward motion. Try throwing a small ball down and catching it. This is the feeling. Stand tall, shoulders down, head up and away, and try this. Don't let your torso become involved. Work for a graceful, comfortable hand position. Turn your hand, palm up, in a welcoming gesture, with fingers comfortably apart, not tense and rounded. Then turn your hand over, palm down. Practice this ictus/rebound with forearms parallel to the floor, hands inside the elbows. Work in patterns of two, three, and four and think about these as moving between ictus points. The word flow is appropriate. To quote Dr. Jordan yet again:

> Rebounds are, essentially, connecting motions between a given pulse and the beat-stroke for the next pulse. The rebound of a standard downbeat moves a distance of 4-6 inches (at *forte*) or perhaps one-third of the height of the conducting frame, slightly to the left of the previous beat-stroke itself—that is, in the direction of the beat to come—and this is a part of the preparation of the second beat. . . . If the music actually sounds first on the second beat, the conductor delivers the first beat as a preparation providing on the beat-stroke of the downbeat. Be careful not to "prepare" the preparatory beat itself.[6]

Practice! Practice! Practice!

Practice is crucial, especially if you have certain conducting problems, such as mixed meter, sections in different tempi, or a particularly difficult rhythmic section. If you have to look down all the time at your music, you have lost vital contact with your people. *They* make the music. *You* evoke the sound. It is a two-way street. The "maestro-mentality" is a myth, as is the "temperamental conductor." Remember, "Temperament is nine-tenths temper."

Stand still and use your frame as a backdrop to your conducting. Align your body, your spine, lift your head up and away, keep your shoulders down, and let the breath literally fall into your body. If you give a definite, music-filled preparation and *you* breathe properly, *they* will come in just fine. Again, to quote Dr. Ann Jones, "Conducting is a series of preparations." We are always ahead. Otherwise we fall into the "There they go, and I must go after them, for I am their leader" syndrome.

I hear you saying, "But with *my* group, I have to initiate the energy, keep it moving, and give out much more than I get back.

If I stand still, and expect them to read my gestures, it will be a pitiful effort." We all know how much effort it takes to get the wheels of a church choir going and keep them moving. No question about it. But, gentle reader, we wear ourselves out, they really don't get much better, and we are like gerbils on an endless wheel, turning around but going nowhere. Here's the deal:

- When you sway (weave, bounce, hop) you do not really hear/listen.
- When you mouth words or sing along, you don't really hear/listen.
- When you grunt (groan, cluck, snap, tap) you don't really hear/listen.

So the questions to ponder become, "What do *they* really sound like? How can I make it better?" Here is the answer! Proper alignment from you, using your body as a backdrop brings results. Looking like the music sounds, letting the sound come to you, receiving the sound, not reaching over into their territory makes for some wonderful results. You can't fix what you don't hear.

Developing nonverbal conducting skills is crucial. Posture, for example, includes the placement of the feet, the movement of the knees, the movement of the head, and body balance. If the conductor's knees are bending, the pitch also sags. Similarly, if the foot, elbows, head, or wrists are keeping time, the primary rhythm is disturbed. It creates an extra focus point for the singers' eyes. The performer must decide which to follow, the foot, the elbow, the head, the wrist, or the hand. Out-of-tune singing can be directly related to the conductor's gestures.

A wonderful dream/nightmare is recounted from a book by J. Timothy Caldwell. In the dream, the conductor walks into a rehearsal with a high school choir that is new to him. This is the first of twenty-five rehearsals he will have to prepare for a concert. He sits down at the piano and begins his usual warm-ups and is immediately elated to hear his ideal sound coming from the choir. He continues the warm-ups and discovers the group can do anything he asks of them technically. He hands out the music, and begins rehearsal with the simplest composition. The choir reads the score with absolute accuracy. He moves to a more difficult piece; again the ensemble reads it accurately. Eventually he has had the ensemble read all the music for the concert, and they have read with unerring accuracy, including the pieces in French and German.

At this point in his dream, he breaks into a cold sweat because for years he has had to teach the rhythms, the pitches, diction, and technique, and now suddenly, he is standing in front of an ensemble that does not have to be taught any of these things! HE HAS TWENTY-FOUR REHEARSALS AND NOTHING TO TEACH![7]

Not to worry, gentle reader. "We" still have plenty to do!

Notes

1. Carl Bamberger, *The Conductor's Art* (New York: McGraw-Hill Book Company, 1965), p. 181.

2. Ray Robinson and Allen Winold, *The Choral Experience: Literature, Materials, and Methods* (San Francisco: Harpercollins College Div., 1976), p. 45.

3. James Jordan, *Evoking Sound* (Chicago: GIA Pubulications, Inc., 1996), p. 69.

4. Ibid.

5. Ibid., pp. 75-76.

6. Ibid.

7. J. Timothy Caldwell, *Expressive Singing: Dalcroze Eurhythmics for Voice* (Upper Saddle River, N.J.: Pearson Education POD, 1994).

CHAPTER SIX

A Dip in the T.U.B.

Ten Ways a Choir Director Can Tell Someone They Can't Sing

1. "I'm sorry, we've run out of robes."

2. "We need strong singers like you in the congregation to help them sing the hymns."

3. "I wouldn't want you to strain your voice."

4. "Did you know singing can aggravate sinus problems?"

5. "You're much too advanced for this choir."

6. "We still need good people for the handbell choir."

7. "It's a shame composers don't write more songs in your style."

8. "You have a unique range—you hit both notes well."

9. "If you join the choir, you'll miss the pastor's new Bible study."

10. "You have excellent posture."

"No one gets a good choir—it has to be built."
Bev Henson

This chapter begins with two stories about warming up.

Story One. Prior to the first rehearsal with a church choir whom I did not know, I was asked, "Do you want me to warm them up?" I foolishly said "yes." Therein ensued some of the worst singing I have ever heard. The warm-up began in C major, and soon everyone was mah-ing, may-ing, and moo-ing all over the place. Forget connected-to-the-breath sound. Forget pitch. Just launch oneself bravely, if inaccurately, at the notes and then be prepared to make music. Be "prepared" to make music? I think not.

Story Two. A world-famous conductor begins with a festival choir, also in C major to warm up. Everyone began to sing in that lower register, and as they ascended, the sound and the pitch carried that heavy register progression forward. In other words, it was out of tune and ugly. Not a religious experience. For the rest of the rehearsal, no one sang in tune even though the conductor, increasingly frustrated, kept after the troops with increasingly less good humor.

The Moral of the Stories

Is there a moral here? Yes! I'm glad you asked. **Never start any warm up, any time, any place, in C major!** That is the moral. The reason, it seems to me, is pretty obvious, but I encounter, on a fairly regular basis, choral groups who begin their warm-ups in what is a lower register, chest register, speaking-voice register for everyone. This is exactly where a person's strongest sound will be since they have been exercising the speaking voice for hours. This is exactly where we should *not* begin vocal warm-ups! To begin in C major and move up by half steps is the worst way to ask people to begin singing together.

I recommend beginning in E-flat major on the fifth (or B-flat) and descending on a neutral vowel: 5-4-3-2-1. Then move up by half steps and continue. Hence the "T" of the word "TUB."

1. Start from the top. We should encourage people to use the top range of the voice, not the speaking voice range. This is not only a healthier way to begin vocalizing, it will also strengthen the other register(s). Beginning in a chest voice register allows for out-of-tune, weighty, dark singing, which does not allow the voice to warm up and usually creates problems for the rest of the rehearsal.

There is a mentality that warming up is just something one goes through, like taking medicine. Often, directors don't know what they hope to accomplish. (How can the singers know, if the director doesn't?) Sometimes, studio vocalises are used that may or may not have group application. A particular vocal exercise used in Madame Slaviansky's studio, will not necessarily be applicable to your choral group.

That first five minutes is vital to the success and viability of your group. It should be done carefully and it should be varied. Now we move on to the "T" in "TUB."

2. Unhinging the jaw. Please, please don't ask your group to "drop" their jaws! "Release" is a much better word. Ask them to place their fingers in that indentation behind their ears and feel the jaw literally "unhinge" as they breathe for singing. Almost everyone I know advocates a singing breath that simulates the beginning of a yawn. The resulting sound should not, however, be a "yawny" one. Imagine the worst bass on your back row with that coming-out-from-the-sewer sound. That is *not* what we want.

3. Breath. Singing would be impossible without the "B" in "TUB." Breathing should be done in combination with unhinging the jaw. Taking a breath for singing is akin to any kind of wind-up and swing. The easiest way for singers to find the "position" is to roll their shoulders back, let them relax, lift the head up and away, and let the breath fall into the body. (See chapter 4.) I have seen directors who had their groups turn to the clock on the wall, take a breath in, then hold it for twenty-five seconds. In my opinion, except for counting to twenty-five, this has no validity whatsoever. It's like walking around the church saying consonants out loud: "Ssss," "Tttt," "Pppp," "Kkkk"—to what purpose is this waste? Consonant articulation without musical context is ludicrous. So is staring at the clock and counting.

Most of our people don't breathe well. They take high, shallow breaths and, as a result, the tone is often high and shallow. Imagine that concept! Encourage your singers to begin in E-flat major on a B-flat, to let the breath fall in, to feel "cool air" in the back of the throat, let the jaw release, and sing a scale passage (5-4-3-2-1) on the sound "YAH" (a yah on each note).

Tuning

Breathing correctly is just the beginning. Even with the breath full and deep, the jaw relaxed, and the connection with the breath made—if, in singing down from 5 to 1, we begin to slip about 3, then we will not produce the sound we desire. Choir warm-ups should also focus on intonation. If we begin our rehearsal with large, ugly, out-of-tune sound, we are asking for trouble throughout the rehearsal. We should start with great vocal energy, but carry the tone lightly and carefully as we descend.

Ask your people to listen. If the pitch sags, sing on numbers and be careful about the 3rd degree of the scale. Ask half of the choir to begin on 1 and ascend to 5 while the other half sings the descending scale pattern. They should "meet" in the middle—a nice way to say "match pitch and be in tune." Something as simple as a five-note scale, with a relaxed jaw and breath connected, really helps your singers learn to phonate properly. They also learn to sing properly. (Sorry, couldn't help myself.)

When we begin on "YAH," we use what William Vennard called the "yawn-sigh" approach. It is very good to ask the choir to begin on that B-flat and slide the "YAH" downward, lightly and finished off with breath—not with a thud at the bottom. They may say, "I cannot slide." Simply reply, "Just do it like you began that last anthem." The feeling then, when you go back to 5-4-3-2-1 is that of continuous air flow, lovely sound, and entry into the choral world that everyone wants to hear.

Generally, I think it is a mistake to buy any vocal warm-up books. Most of the suggested exercises are too difficult and often really don't accomplish what the author desires. If *you* don't have a concept of the vocal sound you want to establish, you won't get it, no matter how many books you buy. Having said that, I do have some favorites that have been helpful.

1. *Sing Legato* by Ken Jennings (Kjos). A lot of us have used this wonderful resource. There is a choral score and an accompaniment score, but I suggest buying only the accompaniment copy. The choir should focus on the desired outcome and it is good for them to have to learn by rote.

2. *The Complete Choral Warm-Up Book* by Russell Robinson and Jay Althouse (Alfred). These guys *do* know what they wish to accomplish and are so bold as to list the suggested vocalises on the right side of the page, accompanied by their suggested use on the left side. These really work.

3. I like to use the collections *Rounds and Canons* and *Where in the World*, both published by Choristers Guild. There are some fun exercises that give some variety.

4. Warm-ups for children! Choristers Guild is a great source of material for teaching and singing. There are many creative articles in *The Chorister*. The Helen Kemp chapter in *Children Sing His Praise* is worth the price of the book.

5. Warm-ups for youth! You can get some good ideas from my little green book, *Building the Youth Choir* (Augsburg-Fortress). For changing voices, the best source is *Working with Adolescent Voices* by John Cooksey (Concordia).

6. The single best, one-book source for vocal technique is *The Diagnosis and Correction of Vocal Faults* by James C. McKinney (Broadman).

General Checklist for Warm-ups
1. Vary the routine.
2. Don't talk about it. Demonstrate, then listen.
3. Never approach this casually or routinely.
4. Don't talk. Demonstrate—listen to them.
5. Use anthem excerpts that lend themselves to a warm-up experience.

6. Use hymn tunes. For example:
   - "Come, Thou Almighty King"—Sing the first line. Pick a comfortable starting pitch, then go up.
   - "All Creatures of Our God and King"—Use the descending "Alleluia."
   - "Come, Christians Join to Sing"—You sing the first part, they respond with "Alleluia, Amen."
7. Say what you expect! For example:
   - "Begin LIGHTLY! As you are coming down, be careful how you sing the 3rd scale step."
   - "Let's do this on numbers, stop on 3, and LISTEN. Half the choir begins on 1, the other half on 5. Meet at 3. Turn and sing this to someone face-to-face and LISTEN."
   - "One half of you sing, the other half listen. Now reverse it and listen."
   - "Don't breathe until you are ready to sing. Put your finger on your sternum bone—make sure the breath 'falls into' your body. Take a cool-air breath. Do you feel cool air in the back of your throat?"

Always encourage—never criticize! Then, begin the rehearsal with something fairly well known that doesn't make great vocal demands. In other words, "How Lovely" from the Brahms *Requiem* is not a good choice. You may sing through the hymns for Sunday, but sing carefully, with good pitch and vowel sounds. There is no excuse for ever allowing a bad vowel into the room. It's just easier to let the good ones hold sway.

And Now, a Word about Rehearsal

I love to rehearse. I'd rather do it than the performance. A good rehearsal is like a symphonic structure for me; an exciting beginning, a peak toward the middle, and a gradual but interesting wind-down. We often try to do too much in each rehearsal since we sing so often in church, and rehearse so seldom. Timing forces one to be honest and not attempt too much. I believe in timing at the start of a rehearsal what it is you hope to accomplish for every anthem. We have to have pieces in various stages of development or we'll get caught. (Just have to put a sidebar here.) That piece for which you need most of the forces? You know, the SSAATTBB one—the one you began announcing six months ago that will be sung on Sunday, the Russian anthem that requires everyone to be present? Save your breath! They won't be there. They *will* be there, however, the following Sunday for that simple two-part anthem by Natalie Sleeth. It is the Murphy's Law of Anthem Planning—never fails. (You know I speak truth.)

Keep a Warm-up List

I am a big basketball and football fan. I love to see the coaches on the sidelines of a football game with their plastic-coated list of plays. They get plenty of money and have lots of assistants, looks like they could remember those plays. I do a similar kind of list so that I have plenty of variety and because I forget from time to time how many there are. My list might look like this:

- Backbone Up and Rib Cage High
- Consonant Caper
- Gregorian Alleluia
- All Together Joyfully Sing
- Viva la Musica[1]

Also on my list are:

- "Blah" (Sing a five-note descending scale.)
- "Hee" (Sing 1-2-3-4-5-4-3-2-1, three times lightly.)
- "America" (Sing the tune of "America" using "doot" or "pahm" *staccato,* then "loo" or "lah" *legato.*

- "Hear it!" (Sing, beginning on F# in unison. High voices move up a half step, low voices move down a half step, and then move back together.)
- "Zing-a-Mama" (Sing Zing-a-Mama, Zing-a-Mama on 5-4-3-2-1, ending with the word Zoo on 1.)
- "Nee-Oh" (Sing Nee-Oh, Nee-Oh, Nee on 5-3-4-2-1.)
- "Nee-Ah" (Sing Nee-Ah, Nee-Ah, Nee on 5-3-4-2-1.)[2]

I always write down the warm-ups in sequence and time them so that they take only five minutes. I know people who warm up for fifteen to twenty minutes, but I think a carefully thought-out warm-up, building toward that first anthem selected, can easily be done in five minutes. Five minutes is a very long time, especially if you DO NOT TALK!

Notes

1. Many of these are Helen Kemp's and may be found in the collections mentioned earlier.

2. Russell Robinson and Jay Althouse, *The Complete Warm-up Book: A Sourcebook for Choral Conductors* (Van Nuys, Calif.: Alfred, 1995).

CHAPTER SEVEN
Give Us a New Song, Alleluia!

> The choir soloist was practicing in the church by the open window. After an hour or so of singing, she stepped outside for a breath of fresh air and noticed the gardener doing some weeding in the bed of roses nearby.
> "How did you like my execution?" the soloist asked.
> The gardener replied, "I'm in favor of it."
>
> • • • • • • • • • • • • • • • • • •
>
> The church soloist was rehearsing for a Sunday service. The choir director and the pianist conferred and then the director said to the singer: "We will start in G minor and then on the third bar, modulate to B major and go into 5/4 meter. When you get to the bridge, modulate back down to F# minor and alternate a 4/4 bar with a 7/4 bar. On the last A section go into double time and slowly modulate back to G minor."
> The singer responds: "Wow! I don't think I can remember all of that."
> The pianist answers: "Well, that's exactly what you did last time!"

Like walking, swimming, snapping fingers, gargling, turning cartwheels, and whistling in the dark, singing is a human potential. The good news is that we do not need any equipment to do it, apart from ourselves. The bad news is that one in four people believe they cannot do it.

We cannot all speak together, but we can all sing together. Anyone who has observed a congregation reading a liturgical prayer for the first time will know the truth of this. Singing has undoubtedly something to do with the emotions, and whether singing makes us feel or feeling makes us sing is a chicken-and-egg argument.

There is a true sense in which we are in danger of seeing the depths of sorrow, anger, and confusion lost from our singing. Those who favor bright choruses tend to shy away from reflecting the shadow side of our emotional spectrum in song, perhaps because they think it is unchristian, or perhaps because they are afraid of aspects of their character yet to be offered to God.[1]

A Story About Hymnal Revision

My letter read, "Dear Dr. Yarrington, at the May 13-14 meeting of the Hymnal Revision Committee (HRC) you were named as a consultant to the Language Sub-Committee. I welcome you to this group." Thus began my odyssey with the revision process of the new *The United Methodist Hymnal,* a journey I found fascinating, exciting, humbling, frustrating, and rewarding.

The mandate of the work, which began in 1984, was to come up with a "model of a new Hymnal." Speaking of that first meeting of the committee, John Lovelace observed: "One thing is for certain about the proposed new hymnal for the United Methodists—it will be small enough to fit into hymnal racks or on the backs of church pews. That's about the only thing known about whatever the book may be called and what it may contain in what sequence. Members of the committee admit to the impossible job of pleasing everyone with a book—or books—to replace the 1965 *Book of Hymns.*" [2]

Dr. Lyle Schaller, church researcher and futurist from Indiana, asserted: "This is probably the most influential committee I have ever met with because it will have the most impact on the denomination. The denomination needs three distinctive marks of identification: (1) a news magazine, which it does not have; (2) a dominant seminary rather than a group of seminaries, and (3) a Hymnal. A hymnal is important because it helps assimilate new persons into a denominational tribe, but only if they recognize something familiar, perhaps something they have learned in another denomination. Denominational loyalty when it comes to buying things like a new hymnal, is not what it used to be." [3]

We have seen every major denomination revise its primary hymnal and many supplements published. There is a treasure of material. Add to that the ever-increasing body of scripture songs, praise songs, worship songs, and we do not lack for material.

We know, from our earlier discussion, that many churches, in their attempt to reach the unchurched, are moving toward services without organs and choirs and hymnals, but with bands and screens and with songs easily assimilated. We know that many classically trained musicians are finding it hard to be in leadership roles for which they feel inadequate. Equally painful is the notion that what they love and have been trained to do in music and liturgy is being called into question daily. Much of the church growth movement seems to devolve on music, which, you remember, was described as the nuclear reactor of congregation participation.

Perhaps one of those "Yarrington Songs" might set the stage for this discussion. You have been waiting for one—right?

> The people who come through your doors at the
>   church
> Are seeking a life-way, for they're on a search
> For meaning, for substance, for heath-filling fare
> "To seek a King"—that's why they are there.
>
> Now junk food is tasty and easy to swallow
> But too much that's sugary can cause one to
>   wallow
> In unwanted fat, getting bigger, not better.
> So here, dear reader is Uncle John's Letter:
>
> To you who must choose what your people
>   will sing,
> I beg for a balance: for to them we bring

The widest and best of our hymn-singing
    treasure.
As new songs and old songs will bring more
    than pleasure.
They satisfy hunger with food that is lasting,
So on to the banquet where no one is fasting.

Who Are the Hymns For?

That is the question, to paraphrase the bard. If one can honestly answer that question, one is a long way toward creative, careful, appropriate hymn choice. The answer is, I believe, the hymns are for the people, for those in the congregation. They should be encouraged to sing, much as Wesley suggested:

DIRECTIONS FOR SINGING

1. Learn these tunes before you learn any others; afterwards learn as many as you please.
2. Sing them exactly as they are printed here, without altering or mending them at all; and if you have learned to sing them otherwise, unlearn it as soon as you can.
3. Sing all. See that you join with the congregation as frequently as you can. Let not a slight degree of weakness or weariness hinder you. If it is a cross to you, take it up, and you will find it a blessing.
4. Sing lustily and with a good courage. Beware of singing as if you were half dead, or half asleep; but lift up your voice with strength. Be no more afraid of your voice now, nor more ashamed of its being heard, than when you sung the songs of Satan.
5. Sing modestly. Do not bawl, so as to be heard above or distinct from the rest of the congregation, that you may not destroy the harmony; but strive to unite your voices together, so as to make one clear melodious sound.
6. Sing in time. Whatever time is sung be sure to keep with it. Do not run before nor stay behind it; but attend close to the leading voices, and move therewith as exactly as you can; and take care not to sing too slow. This drawling way

naturally steals on all who are lazy; and it is high time to drive it out from us, and sing all our tunes just as quick as we did at first.

7. Above all sing spiritually. Have an eye to God in every word you sing. Aim at pleasing him more than yourself, or any other creature. In order to do this attend strictly to the sense of what you sing, and see that your heart is not carried away with the sound, but offered to God continually; so shall your singing be such as the Lord will approve here, and reward you when he cometh in the clouds of heaven.

From John Wesley's *Select Hymns*, 1761

So, if the hymns are for the congregation, who are they not for?

- **The Pastor.** To indulge personal preference or choose from limited experience and knowledge.
- **The Organist.** To display pyro-technique, reharmonize or move up by half steps at will.
- **The Choir Director.** To "raise" the standards of the congregation by choosing only "good" hymns.
- **The Congregation.** To only sing the ones "they know."

But, you said, the hymns are for the congregation. Yes, gentle reader, but the truth is that the hymns are for all God's people. I always found it helpful when on a church staff to let the ministers know up front that I did not consider the hymns my purview. As a "servant-musician," I felt that many needs could be met if those who had the responsibility of choice were sensitive and adopted a broad view. If the music director knows his or her hymnal well, he or she is in a good position to make suggestions for alternative selection. Most of the time, musicians tend to be skeptical about hymns classified as "gospel" hymns, probably because people seem to enjoy them too much. The same statement might be made about praise songs and the like.

If the decision making could be approached in light of the most "appropriate" song instead of a self-appointed notion of what is "right," or worse, "good" or "bad," I believe we would help ourselves in the worship wars. Again, John Bell has some wonderful insight:

We all know what bad leadership is like:

The guitarists who arrive when most people are already gathered, then strut about self-importantly tuning up, testing the microphones, making gruff comments to each other, all in full view of the congregation.

The organist who never practices the hymns, but who insists on playing them very loudly whether the text is about sorrow and death or joy and resurrection, and who refuses to play contemporary percussive song on the piano.

The worship leader who patronizes the choir and musicians by telling them how good "that" was, even when "that" was awful, but who would never dream of saying an encouraging word to the congregation.

The choir whose altos and sopranos amble in with huge handbags, which one presumes must contain secret love letters, bank statements and hereditary jewelry, and who take deep offence when they are asked to vacate their sacred space for one service so that children can present a play.

The soloist who has spent more time in front of the mirror than on his/her knees, and who, as if cantoring or singing a solo were insufficient, insists on bawling his/her guts out during every congregational song, just in case people forget that he/she is there.[4]

I do not wish to do a disservice to this fine book, but I will summarize what I think are several salient points regarding communication. Bell says that, in the ambiguity of communication there are (1) musical ambiguity; (2) the tune; and (3) textual ambiguity. (Please read the entire book—I commend it to you.)

1. Musical Ambiguity: That is, different aspects of sound produce in us positive, negative, or ambivalent resonances; the instrument or voice articulating the music, the style of the music or any discernible tune. He mentions the sight and sound of bagpipes, which "fills some people with patriotic fervor and others with instant revulsion." The same may be said for guitars in church. "In such instances, people are reacting negatively or positively, not to what is about to happen, but to what in the past has happened concerning the instrument in view."

2. The Tune: "Tunes carry with them memories from the past—from where we were when we first heard this piece, of who was playing it, of whether or not it was a good experience. And all that experience from the past colors our appreciation in the present. . . . Our ears are not neutral. They are conditioned by what they have heard in the past, and the associations that gather around certain instruments, styles, and melodies affect for good or ill how we respond to new material we listen to."

3. Textual Ambiguity: Bell continues: "When we read words, we never do so neutrally, but color their contemporary meaning through their past significance in our lives. Language is a powerful tool for controlling or liberating people, and in the song of the church it can include, exclude or antagonize. We are surely children of God, but we are equally creatures of our conditioning. To distinguish between the one and the other requires sometimes honesty, sometimes integrity, and sometimes humble heroism."[5]

Give Us a New Song, Alleluia!

I love the idea of singing both new and old songs. We are called in the chorus to the kind of inclusivity of which John Bell speaks and about which I believe the church is called. We are also called, in this chorus, to praise Jesus with our heart, body, breath, bone, and mind and to follow him alone.

It is not enough to welcome with words but to embrace with hospitality all who come. We encourage their active participation, we recognize the differing tribes represented, but we maintain our meaningful traditions, which include liturgical models in prayer, creed, and song.

To argue that we must give up the Lord's Prayer because a "seeker" doesn't know it, is abrogating responsibility to equip those who come. To print words only, never using the hymnal, can be exclusionary rather than contemporary. When I attend such a service, I really don't know the songs and, while willing to learn and join in, I feel what those less-churched probably do when the songs come out of the hymnal.

Most of the major denominations have revised their primary hymnal and have, in addition, published supplement after supplement. There is an explosion of new texts and tunes. Part of our job is to choose wisely for "everyone who comes." For me, the Holy Trinity of choosing hymns is: (1) variety, (2) balance, and (3) that which is most appropriate.

Sometimes a chorus, easily learned, is what is needed. A simple, well-known refrain or a familiar excerpt from a hymn may fill the bill. I believe that, in our attempt to reach others for Christ, we narrow down the musical possibilities instead of broadening them. Why? Is it because "they" might not like us or not come back? I believe we sell those people short and are not courageous enough to lead and teach in winsome ways.

Every Kind Of Song—For Everyone Who Comes

This could be a worship mantra. Repeat it to yourself. Say it out loud!

- **Pastors:** Are you willing to expand your horizons in song and text, allowing every kind of song to be sung?
- **Organists:** Are you willing to accompany on the piano when the song calls for it?
- **Choir Directors:** Are you willing to stand up and teach and lead every kind of song with expectation, grace, humility and hospitality?
- **Choirs:** Are you willing to embrace your primary role, that of leading congregational singing?

Hear Our Prayer

When (not if) someone comes to your church needing to talk, are we ready? Does our worship provide avenues for listening, working, and caring? Mostly, I suspect, we "hush the song" or the "smell" or the "look." Jesus hung out with all the wrong people, which makes great reading but is pretty hard to emulate.

Can worship and song and liturgy really convey God's love to someone needy to hear? I believe with my whole heart that it can—that we can—but only if we are willing to be servants, not masters. We must be willing to let songs be sung that we do not even like—or worse, love to malign. No harm is done by singing "I Come to the Garden" if it is the most appropriate song for the moment. Much harm has been done by gathering our robes about us and raising our noses in the snob position. Hear me, ye musicians! Come down from your lofty perches and join in the fray. Hear me, ye pastors! Your people are hurting and needy. Can you expand your horizons to allow more and different songs to be sung? You get the point. If we intend to praise Jesus with all our body, breath, bone, and mind, we'd better be about it. Our people, gathered and blended, woven and spliced are waiting.

Notes

1. John L. Bell, *The Singing Thing: A Case for Congregational Singing* (Chicago: GIA Publications, Inc., 2000), p. 13.

2. From "What Gift Can We Bring: A Pastoral Musician Looks at *The United Methodist Hymnal,*" an article written in the summer of 1982 by John Yarrington.

3. Ibid.

4. Bell, *The Singing Thing,* p. 13.

5. Ibid., pp. 141-51.

CHAPTER EIGHT

Never Look at the Trombones

---

1. What's the difference between a bass trombone
   and a chain saw?
   Vibrato.

2. What is a gentleman?
   *Somebody who knows how to play the trombone,
   but doesn't.*

3. How many trombonists does it take to change
   a lightbulb?
   Just one, but he'll do it too loudly.

4. What is the dynamic range of the bass trombone?
   On or off.

"Never look at the trombones, it only encourages them."
Richard Straus

"We cannot expect you to be with us all the time, but perhaps you could be good enough to keep in touch now and again."   *Sir Thomas Beecham to a musician during a rehearsal*

"I never use a score when conducting my orchestra.
Does a lion tamer enter a cage with a book on how to tame a lion?"   *Dimitri Mitropolous*

"Already too loud!"
*Bruno Walter at his first rehearsal with an American orchestra,
on seeing the players reaching for their instruments*

In an earlier chapter, I confessed my passion for conducting. I want my students who leave here to be conductors, not "choral" conductors or "orchestral" conductors. Only in America do we make that distinction anyway. Unfortunately, those of us who believe in the art of conducting—whether choral or orchestral or combination of both—are often tarred with the brush, usually by instrumentalists, of being a "choral" conductor. This is definitely not a term of endearment.

I was fortunate to have a cellist who took me under her wing, often sliced off sizable portions of my skin, but taught me about working with an orchestra. It is so very different from working with a choir. And, because I wanted to conduct the wonderful literature available for choir and orchestra, I learned. I spent much time offstage at orchestral rehearsals observing, then going on stage during the break to see what "they" were actually seeing in their parts. I saw professional conductors who moved around a lot and didn't seem to have much connection in the way they looked to the actual music being played and/or sung. I decided early on, that, since I wasn't brilliant, I would have to study like mad and be able to give clear, concise gestures. It worked. Now, I try to teach the same to my students.

The best conducting book I know is *Face to Face with an Orchestra*. It details clearly the mentality and expectation of an orchestra and has been most helpful, particularly to beginning students. I am also indebted to Bev Henson, who taught many of us how to pull together the various orchestral and choral threads to make a whole. I lost some skin there, as well.

When instrumentalists come to play for you at church, I think they come with a prejudice already in place, and undergirded by much bad experience. They have played for conductors in church who flailed away with nary a discernible downbeat, and choirs unaccustomed to singing with orchestral accompaniment, so they get used to conductors who gesture, waiting for the orchestra to play, which usually means that the whole thing slows down, sometimes even stops. Yes, they are being paid. Why would they suffer through this? The obvious answer is because they need the money—and we all know about the extravagant salaries paid to those of us in the music business.

I think that, in spite of this well-oiled prejudice, they always hope it will be better. When they encounter a conductor who does not get in their way, and a choir who actually has been trained to sing on the downbeat, they are pleasantly surprised, and you will find, that they will play better and better for you and your choir.

So, here are some possible scenarios:

Anthem with Solo Instrument (Scenario #1)

- Do not assume anything, even if you hire a player.
- Give attention first in the rehearsal to the instrumentalist. Often a conductor never even looks, much less cares.
- Take time to tune.
- Know about transposing instruments.

Anthem with Brass or String Quartet (Scenario #2)

- Do not assume anything. The local award-winning Rooster Band, from which you have extracted a brass quartet, has rehearsed all year on the three pieces they take to contest. They take endless minutes tuning. They may not sight-read very well (probably not, actually) and you would be well advised to go to the school, if possible, and rehearse separately with them. They agree to the "gig" and love the pay, but may skip the step to look at the music before they come.
- After they are with your choir, give attention to them first. Play and sing through the anthem or cantata without stopping—without talking.
- Adjust balance. A choir can be more precise, use consonants better; brass can play into their stands and they *can* play softer. The less-experienced players, of course, have less dynamic control. Be prepared.
- If you are using strings, meet with the concert master

(mistress) ahead of time. Sing what you want. This person will be invaluable in getting it for you. Learn about bowing so you can ask for an up-bow or a down-bow. Don't try to tell them how to play because they probably know better than you do. Do insist on accurate rhythms, proper pitches, and good intonation. If they are not together, simply stop and say, "We are not together. Could we do this again." In spite of every bad experience, they would like to be part of something musical and wonderful. Go with that idea. Remember that the viola is in a different clef and one of them may ask, "Do we have a D in measure 13?" Probably they know they do, but they just want to see if you do. It's a little orchestral game. Better be ready.

Chamber or Full Orchestra (Scenario #3)

- Your score study is essential. Start from the big picture and work into smaller units. Find out how the piece is scored. Get some help if you need it. There is no shame in working with a more experienced conductor. There is great shame in standing in front of an orchestra with little knowledge of what could happen.

- Make a graph of the work as a whole with text noted, key relationships, time of each movement, instruments used.

- The orchestra members will bless you if you arrange the rehearsal so as to use the most players first, then let those not needed go.

- If you have hired a union orchestra, there are rules to follow about how much time you have and how many breaks they have. A good contractor will take care of a lot of this for you, but you have to know how it works.

- Make sure what the singers and players have in the way of numbers or letter names or both. Nothing is so deadly to a rehearsal as the question, "Orchestra, do you have numbers or letters?" You need to check the full score with the parts to see if there are any discrepancies here. Time well spent in advance of the rehearsal means you can concentrate and use all of the resources available.

- Look at the individual parts to see what "they" see. If you have particular articulation in the choral parts (and you should) this must be duplicated in the orchestral parts either by bowing or by articulation in the case of winds, brass, or percussion.
- Meet with the concert master. It is money well spent.
- Know how long the entire work is and how long each movement is. After a complete run-through, without stopping (and without talking) have several designated places from which to start. Don't facilitate or hesitate, say, "Let's begin in the second movement, bar 26." That will help you get over your nerves at this large amount of sound coming right at you.
- Don't scrimp on what you need in the orchestra. Three violins make a better section than two. Sometimes there is a reduced orchestration provided by the composer that really works. However, hiring two trumpets when the score calls for three, and asking the organist to play the third part (actually happened but not to me) is not a good idea. Cost may dictate choice of work. There are many fine pieces that do not take the full orchestral forces. Bigger works not only require bigger orchestral forces but more "horsepower" vocally and soloistically.

Protocol for Working with an Orchestra

There is a protocol for working with an orchestra. I am not going to repeat the information in *Face to Face with an Orchestra*, but encourage you to get the book and read it.

- Be clear in your gestures. At first, pay almost all attention to the orchestra. Listen. Do not get overwhelmed with all the sound coming at you.
- Play and sing through. Don't stop; don't talk. The

orchestra needs to know what is involved, to see the entire work, and often, they will correct their own mistakes on a second run-through.

- Only after an initial run, can you begin to refine.
- Ask for what you want: shorter/longer, *legato/staccato*, softer/louder, more marked/more separation.
- Sing what you want to the orchestra with all the color, nuance, shading, you desire. Let the concert master suggest bowing to accomplish what you wish. Give them time to mark.
- Make sure the orchestra knows the order of movements and if any are cut. Are you doing the repeats as in the score?
- If you plan to give a full measure before a movement or if you tell the orchestra, "I will direct this in two" you better do it. Don't say "in two" and then direct "in four." Your study and practice should make all of this secure. Your careful marking reminds you, especially when you are nervous, of what you intend to accomplish.
- Be respectful, but definite.
- Make an orchestral seating with individual names and keep in front of you. When you want something more or different from the first or second oboe player, call them by name, "John, could you give a bit more articulation there." You will be amazed how much difference this makes.
- Rarely can the orchestra sit in a usual configuration. Often, they have to sit to the right and left of the conductor rather than in a usual setup. Be sure that the people who usually sit together are together, even if they have be two behind two.
- Two violins do not a section make. Three is always better.
- Train the choir to over-do the consonants, put some ahead of the beat (PR–aise, GLO–ry, BL–st, CH–rist) and teach them to be "with the stick." You will be farther away than

usual and the more they respond to your clear gestures with the stick, the better performance you will have.

Your part, O conductor, is to study well, rehearse well, and deliver the musical goods. In other words, *conduct yourselves accordingly.*

CHAPTER NINE

The Spiritual Life of the Church Musician

After a hardy West Virginia rainstorm filled all the potholes in the streets and alleys, a young mother watched her two little boys playing in the puddle through her kitchen window. The older of the two, a five-year-old lad, grabbed his sibling by the back of his head and shoved his face into the water hole. As the boy recovered and stood laughing and dripping, the mother ran to the yard in a panic.

"Why on earth did you do that to your little brother?" she chided the older boy in anger.

"We were just playing 'church,' Mommy!" he said. "I was baptizing him in the name of the Father, the Son, and in the hole he goes!"

People who do not work within the church may believe that pastors, choir directors, and other church leaders have an easier time maintaining a spiritual focus than laypersons out "in the world." But the church is comprised of ordinary people who make mistakes and are in constant need of forgiveness. Yes, it is often hard to be spiritual while doing the Lord's work.

An "It's Hard to Be Spiritual" Checklist

✓ It's hard to be spiritual when you are on a church staff.

✓ It's hard to be spiritual when you provide "musical services."

✓ It's hard to be spiritual when you are the "worship manager."

✓ It's hard to be spiritual when there is no time for reading, reflection, or study.

✓ It's hard to be spiritual when the world calls the tune.

1. It's hard to be spiritual when you are on a church staff. This is the "you went to seminary and therefore you pray" syndrome. Or the "could you just lead a few songs as people gather, since you went to conservatory" syndrome. I am always looking for a group into which I could merge without having to bring the prayer or lead the song. An organization called "Men Alive" has been wonderful for me. I went, needing spiritual nourishment and fellowship, but not wanting a position of leadership. I didn't even have to play the piano (imagine!) for the first year—until the faithful keyboard person faltered. Now I am doing just that—but ONLY that!

2. It's hard to be spiritual when you are providing "musical services." Paul Westermeyer maintains that church musicians are perceived as those responsible for creating musical services that keep the congregation happy, or simply to "give everybody warm fuzzies."[1] This presents two intolerable tensions. First, if a congregation is truly Christian and not a reflection of the culture, its musicians will feel the gnawing sense that simply meeting people's needs is wrong. Second, church musicians will still feel pressured to satisfy the desires of every person in the congregation.

3. It's hard to be spiritual when you are the worship manager. "Worship Manager" is a term used by Harold Best to describe two types of management of worship. The first is a "careful, rational, and patterned construct of all the good and proper things of which high culture, liturgical protocols, and mannered methodologies are a part." The second is "behaviorally and contextually managed and on the surface, purported to avoid formalism and to thrive on the spontaneous. It is supposedly less calculated, but it is nevertheless carefully managed, even staged."[2] The church musician must find a balance between these two styles of leadership, and still acknowledge the constant guidance of the Holy Spirit in worship planning.

4. It's hard to be spiritual when there is no time for reading, reflection, or study. Endless meetings, memos, and minutia crowd our days. There are budgets meetings, staff meetings, committee meetings, "brainstorming" sessions, staff retreats, and constant spur-of-the-moment interruptions in the church musician's schedule. Church musicians must plan for quiet devotion, prayer, and Bible study along with routine, everyday tasks.

5. It's hard to be spiritual when the world calls the tune. Harold Best believes that church music today is in a "deep and whirling quandary, a kid of noisesomely troubled busyness. . . . Church leaders [are] trying to make musical decisions based on aesthetic capacities the size of gooseberries, moral turpitude mixed with musicological wizardry, mass-produced junk by dozens of composers whose royalties are in five figures."[3] Perhaps this seems overstated, but Dr. Best gets to the heart of a condition he describes as "symptomatic of a profound disjunction." The first two verses in Romans 12 describe two diametrically opposed systems:

> I appeal to you therefore, brothers and sisters, by the mercies of God, to present your bodies as a living sacrifice, holy and acceptable to God, which is your spiritual worship. (Rom. 12:1)

> Do not be conformed to this world but be transformed by the renewing of your minds, so that you may discern what is the will of God—what is good and acceptable and perfect. (Rom. 12:2)

Dr. Best explains: "I believe we have largely conformed to this world, not because we have borrowed its music—and that we surely have—but because we seem to be mesmerized by its world view, so much so that it has become almost one with our piety." [4]

The Tension Between Music and Ministry

In all my years as a church musician, there has been an incredible tension between the demands of ministry and those of music making. I have been bashed for using the word *per-*

formance, and criticized for working on good vowels, crisp consonants, intonation, phrasing, and other elements of musicality and choral hygiene. I believe that musical standards need not be sacrificed in the name of ministry. I also believe that ministry need not be sacrificed in the name of musical standards. I know that tension. The more one challenges the best performance possible, the more one is open to the notion that this is an ego trip and has nothing to do with church music. As if the product doesn't matter—only the intent.

Protect Time for Bible Study and Reflection

I begin each day with Bible reading and prayer. Here are some guidelines that have been helpful to me.

1. Be aware of the Living Christ. Focus on one of the following scriptures; try to "live your way into it." See if you get any new grasp of what the "presence" can mean. (Read Luke 24:13-15; John 10:7-15; John 20:11-18; Acts 6:15; 7:54-60; Galatians 2:20.)

2. Confess to our Lord and listen for his response. This is a time for soul searching. As a means of dealing with your sins, select one of the following passages. Remember, it is God's yardstick by which we are measured. (Read Psalm 51; Matthew 4:1-11; John 3:1-15; John 18:25-27; Romans 3:23; 5:12; 1 Timothy 1:15.)

3. Hear again God's call, renew an old call, or be led in a new direction. (Read Genesis 12:1-3; Exodus 3:1-12; Isaiah 6:1-13; Jeremiah 1:4-10; Jonah 1:1-3; Luke 5:27-29; Matthew 4:18-22; John 15:12-17; Acts 16:6-10.)

4. Fellowship with other believers. Cultivate relationships with church members whose spirituality you recognize and whose trust you value. Keep in touch with other colleagues and nurture them as well. You don't have to be alone! (Read Exodus 17:8-12; 1 Kings 19:14-18; Hebrews 10:24-25; Luke 9:28-36; Matthew 26:36-46; Philippians 4:10-18.)

Humor Is a Worthy Comrade

Why humor? Why laughter? In a recent article in *Church Music Workshop*, William Willimon reflects on this question: "We laugh because something is ludicrous, surprising, unexpected, absurdly incongruous. . . . Life has a way of bringing the absurd, the surprising, the incongruous to us."[5] Every choir director knows this to be true and learns to expect the unexpected!

Humor also keeps us from taking ourselves too seriously. When we are able to laugh at ourselves, we recognize that we are not in control. We can celebrate our joys, but we can also acknowledge our limitations. And humor turned toward the podium is often helpful in easing tension—ours, or somebody's else's. The healing effects of laughter are well known. Scripture teaches that "a cheerful heart is a good medicine, but a downcast spirit dries up the bones" (Prov. 17:22). Offering the gift of humor first to ourselves, and then to a world-weary congregation, is a sacred privilege. C. S. Lewis wisely acknowledged: "Joy is the serious business of heaven!" [6]

Notes

1. Paul Westermeyer, "The Practical Life of the Church Musician" in *The Christian Century* (September 1989).

2. Harold Best, "Is the Twentieth Century Too Late?" from an unpublished manuscript.

3. Ibid.

4. Ibid.

5. William H. Willimon quoted in *Church Music Workshop: Practical Tools for Effective Music Ministry* (September–December 2002): 4.

6. C. S. Lewis, *Letters to Malcolm: Chiefly on Prayer* (London: Geoffrey Bles, 1964).

Suggested Reading

Bell, John L. *The Singing Thing: A Case for Congregational Singing*. Chicago: GIA Publications, 2000.

Best, Harold. *Music Through the Eyes of Faith*. San Francisco: Harper, 1993.

Cooksey, John. *Working with Adolescent Voices*. St. Louis, Mo.: Concordia Publishing House, 1999.

Dawn, Marva. *A Royal Waste of Time*. Grand Rapids: William B. Eerdmans, 1999.

———. *To Walk and Not Faint: A Month of Meditations on Isaiah 40*. Grand Rapids: William B Eerdmans, 1997.

Demaree, Robert W. and Don V. Moses. *The Complete Conductor,* Englewood Cliffs: Prentice-Hall, 1995.

Deschner, Roger. *Your Ministry of Singing in the Church*. Nashville: Discipleship Resources, 1990.

Doran, Carol and Thomas Troeger. *Trouble at the Table: Gathering the Tribes for Worship*. Nashville: Abingdon Press, 1992.

Jennings, Kenneth. *Sing Legato*. San Diego: Kjos, 1982.

Jordan, James. *Evoking Sound: Body Mapping Principles and Basic Conducting*. Chicago: GIA Publications, Inc., 1996.

———. *The Musician's Soul: A Journey Examining Spirituality for Performers, Teachers, Composers, and Music Educators*. Chicago: GIA Publications, Inc., 1999.

Long, Thomas G. *Beyond the Worship Wars: Building Vital and Faithful Worship*. The Alban Institute, 2001.

McKinney, James C. *The Diagnosis and Correction of Vocal Faults*. Nashville: Broadman, 1982.

Moses, Don, Robert Demaree, Jr., and Allen Ohmes. *Face to Face with an Orchestra*. Princeton, N.J.: Prestige Publications, 1987.

Neuen, Donald, *Choral Concepts*. Wadsworth/Thompson Learning, 2002. See especially the following chapters: "8. Score Preparation and Analysis"; "9. Rehearsals and Auditions"; and "11. Artistic Musical Conducting."

Nouwen, Henri J. M. *The Wounded Healer: Ministry in a Contemporary Society*. New York: Doubleday, 1979.

Palmer, Parker J. *The Courage to Teach: Exploring the Inner Landscape of a Teacher's Life*. San Francisco: Jossey-Bass, Inc., Publishers, 1997.

Robinson, Russell and Jay Althouse. *The Complete Choral Warm-Up Book: A Sourcebook for Choral Conductors*. Van Nuys, Calif.: Alfred, 1995.

Rotermund, Donald, ed. *Children Sing His Praise: A Handbook for Children's Choir Directors*. Concordia Publishing House, 1986.

Up Front! Becoming the Complete Choral Conductor. Boston: ECS Publishing, Boston. This is multiauthor work. See especially: "Score Selection, Study, and Interpretation" (Gordon Paine); "Conducting" (Donald Neuen); "Choral Tone" (Paul Brandvik); and "The Tools of a Choral Musician" (Guy B. Webb).

Yarrington, John. *Building the Youth Choir: Training and Motivating Teenage Singers*. Augsburg Fortress, 1990.

————. *Somebody's Got My Robe*. Nashville: Abingdon Press, 1997.